RETURN
TO
CENTER

The Flowering of Self-Trust

BOBBIE PROBSTEIN

Photographs by the Author

January 2004
For Olive:
I love and honor
you so very deeply!
Love, Bobbie

DEVORSS & COMPANY
P.O. BOX 550, MARINA DEL REY, CA 90294-0550

3rd Printing, 1990

ISBN: 0-87516-554-0
Library of Congress Catalog Card Number: 85-70723

DeVorss & Company, Publisher
P.O. Box 550
Marina del Rey, CA 90294

Printed in The United States of America

Acknowledgments

I am grateful to Phyllis Eisenberg, Bette Albracht, Pat van Rhyn, Janet Sandell and Carol Bellin for their weekly literary critique. Their continuous support, encouragement and love helped birth this child I call *Return to Center.*

Jane Schoenberg eased the birth pains in many ways: her friendship and editing talents deserve recognition.

Hedda Lark, at DeVorss, helped with her ability to solve problems and clarify issues.

My appreciation extends to Arthur Levy, Bobbie Lippman, Paul Abell and Tricia Kelly for their perceptive comments.

A special "thank you" to three of the finest metaphysical teachers I have known: Brugh Joy, Hal Stone, and Thelma Moss, who took the time from their busy schedules to read the manuscript and offer constructive suggestions.

And for my family—Larry, Lindy and Denny—who nourished this child inside me, I offer my book as a testament to trusting the love within us.

Introduction

Our world needs consciousness. More than anything else, greater than any other priority, our world needs consciousness. It needs people who know who they are and what motivates them, so they can make clear choices about their lives.

Entering into the consciousness process is remarkably varied. Once having entered this process, however, there is no turning back. There is within us a fire that thirsts for greater consciousness, a fire as strong and as passionate as any other basic instinctual energy matrix. *Return to Center* is the story of that fire, how it manifested in one woman, and what she did with it.

The process of becoming conscious varies greatly, but there is a general theme to the journey. We must discover that within each of us lives an amazing array of different parts, and we need to learn how they interact with the parts in others. Embracing our many selves is a challenging, courageous and exciting process! Boredom lessens as the thirst for understanding ourselves increases, for we humans are incredibly complex and the self-exploration takes us into some amazing spaces.

Bobbie's journey began in a rather innocent way: she took a class in self-hypnosis. Out of this beginning, the unconscious gradually began to open, and one day she tuned in to an unknown inner voice. It was quite childlike, but as she let it speak, remarkable insights emerged. Bobbie was in touch with her first "inner teacher;" she had inadvertently begun the process described by C. G. Jung as Active Imagination.

The other ingredient that marked the beginning of Bobbie's journey was a wise and supportive teacher. Over and over again, we see the role of significant teachers in her life, as she moves toward greater self-awareness and empowerment.

Her story is not all happy. It carries the pain and difficulty of a primary relationship, and the conflict that is so profound for so many of us: how do we live with another and at the same time maintain our own identity?

Return to Center is not just a personal story. It is a deep teaching about consciousness and how it develops. Watching Bobbie go through her experiences gives us the picture of her gradual empowerment, her developing ability to help other people support the transformational process in themselves. It is the story of how a planetary teacher develops.

Bobbie does not espouse "A Way" or "A Path." What she instills is the love of process, the excitement of new discoveries, and the courage to stay with whatever reality belongs to her at the moment. It is a chronicle of our times that cannot help but warm each of us as we proceed along our respective paths.

Hal Stone, Ph.D.

Los Angeles, California

Dedicated with love
to my father,
Jack Slote,
who has taught me the meaning
of integrity and courage.

When I began this book
it was a casual attempt to record
some metaphysical and healing experiences.
I was unused to such things;
my focus was on husband and home,
children and friends.
I could not understand why I,
skeptical and agnostic,
would have such events in my life,
but it seemed important to me to frame them
with words, to keep them forever fresh and renewable.
Then my life changed dramatically . . . not in the way I
wished, but the way it was.
In one year's span I had no marriage,
no home, no children who needed me.
In the tearing pain of separations, of endings,
and the fear of new beginnings,
my greatest support
was my inner voice writing
page after page about me from a far
different perspective,
attuned to a different vibration.
But this is no 'sweet' story;
it is a painfully human narrative
of a profound and profane woman, who acknowledges
with love and appreciation a multitude
of friends, teachers, and family,
and finds no separation in their many roles
in her blessed life.

Contents

Definitions

metaphysics: the branch of philosophy concerned with the ultimate nature of existence. The principal area of metaphysical speculation is the study of the ultimate nature of being.

metaphysical: beyond the physical or material; incorporeal, supernatural or transcendental.

parapsychology: the study of mental phenomena not explainable by accepted principles of science.

paranormal: beyond the range of scientifically known or recognizable phenomena.

consciousness: the totality of one's thoughts, feelings and impressions.

Sources: The New Columbia Encyclopedia; Funk & Wagnall's New Standard Dictionary of the English Language; Webster's New World Dictionary.

PART ONE

PHENOMENA

Lifeboat

March, 1981: It is six months since Larry and I have separated, after twenty-eight and one-half years of marriage. We've come to Honolulu, to see if we can talk our way out of the impasse and perhaps recapture some of the joy we once shared.

The phone rings. It is obviously his girl friend; he turns away to speak briefly to her, hangs up the telephone and looks at me. It rings again. Angry and helpless, I begin to cry.

He leaves the room, leaves sadly, watching me crying. Fifteen minutes later, he calls from downstairs to say that he loves me. I see the faint imprint of her number on the yellow pad of paper by the telephone. Does he call and say he loves her too? Is the intonation, the vibrant voice, the same for her as it is for me?

I sit on the high balcony of my hotel room in this cemented paradise and see the persistent bank of dark grey clouds roiling over the mountain tops. Almost anywhere else in the world it would mean rain. Here, the trade winds blow them back with unseen force, and only gentle wisps of clouds escape the pressure to drift and cast their softening shadows on land and

3

sea. The harbor below me and to my left reflects the stick shapes of boats going nowhere, tied to the dock. Boats waiting to be directed by man-force and wind-force, having no will of their own. And I? I've managed to stay afloat in my stormy sea, and know through the pain that I'm no longer drifting. I am my own lifeboat now, outfitted with a strong rudder, a small sail, and enough nourishment to take me into the sheltering arms of the snug harbor that I sense is just beyond my horizon line. I know it is a new land, a green and luminous one, peopled by friendly inhabitants who do not lie or cheat. It's a real and possible paradise, this one . . . not the hallucination of a starved and lonely sailor.

I sit alone for hours and see little, although I am aware of city forms and park shapes and sea colors. They all mean nothing, for at this moment I'm an empty shell hearing my own sea-changes, uncoiling and breaking the tangled lines that have held me and kept me from moving swiftly toward the loving port I know is my destination.

Where have I been, that it has taken me so long to chart a course?

Forty-eight years of growing, over twenty-eight of them married to one man; mother of two girls, now women; only child of two adoring parents; a person of some talents for loving, living, healing; a woman wrapped in a reasonably attractive package that is slightly worn but not destroyed; a woman of wisdom, able at last to hear her own strong voice above the wind.

I pour some coffee. A dove alights on the railing, coos softly, cocks its white head and stares at me with one unblinking eye. It flies away, looking for crumbs of nourishment on another level. I get up and move to the edge to watch its graceful, looping flight. Far below I see colorful, rigid forms of swimming pools, tennis courts, fountain. I see people moving slowly, soundlessly. From up here they remind me of snails. Do we weave an invisible, silvery trail of our passage in this world? Twelve years ago, mine might have ended in a splatter on the cement below me: living seemed not worth the pain.

I, who had everything, so I thought, suddenly had nothing, so I believed. The man I adored had found another woman, and was enmeshed in his passion for her, all the while denying it to me. He turned away from my warmth in our bed. We separated then for ten days.

Thank God for the children. If it hadn't been for my responsibility and love for them, I might have done it, might have done myself in. The temptation to be out of pain was that strong, that powerful. Instead, an analyst tried to be helpful and gave me advice and tranquilizers and sleeping pills that made me dizzy and weak but did not stop the hurricane-force feelings of anger and fear and anguish at being lied to and abandoned.

Why did I stay? I loved him still, and had not the vision to see that I could ever want anyone else or that anyone might want me.

His love affair ended, and once again we promised each other the world. With soft voice and warm brown eyes, he said, "You're my whole world, sweetheart." I believed him, thought we'd be OK forever with the big crisis behind us. There were so many special times, joyous times, when I lay in his arms and counted myself the luckiest woman in the whole world: in love with and loved by a man so surpassingly wonderful. He was my life.

Time laid its cool hands on my shoulders and gradually eased the burden of grief I carried.

Something has happened to the trade winds. The sky is no longer blue. Grey, fat clouds are merging and billowing, and the air feels thick with change.

There is a soft hissing as the rain begins. A slick, slippery sound as the cars slide over shining streets. No wind at all. The flags droop listlessly on their silver poles, as though they have given up all hope of flying again. I feel the rain on my face and stick out my tongue to lap it in, and laugh and laugh and laugh. Somewhere between my throat and heart it turns into a cry, and warm salt tears merge with the cool spring rain and fall to the terrace.

*   *   *

When the girls were teenagers, a new surge of life began to grow in me as surely as a fetus stirs in a womb. But it was not like anything I had ever known or read about; some unconscious but nurturing force in me protected us, and it thrived through my doubt and neglect. No nine-month baby, this, but eons in the making, years in which my child-like explorations of psychic phenomena, healing, and energy transfers became stronger and more directed by this inner child, so much wiser than my brain. The unborn but vocal force is *'Paul.'* I know it at last for what it is: my inner wisdom struggling to emerge; my connection to the Father, the Source. My test in trusting.

The rain stops. The pain stops. The grey ocean is replaced by a blue, shining one. The harbor reflects the golden sun once more and a rainbow, tentative and pale, arches from the horizon to a passing ship.

Mindpower

Ten years earlier, I found my inner voice through an elementary course in self-hypnosis.

I was skeptical that it would work for me, but curiosity impelled me to enroll. Since leaving college nearly twenty years before, to get married, I'd almost always taken a class of some kind, usually in the fine arts field.

I wasn't at all clear about what self-hypnosis actually was: it sounded mysterious, dramatic, and intriguing. I only knew that I'd be willing to learn anything that could help me get rid of allergies, and—more important—I was *not* willing to trust someone else to play with my mind. I'd read a lot of scary stories about that. My skepticism would be my protection.

The teacher, Jim Takacs, was a personable man of enormous vitality, and I listened intently. He captured my interest immediately by expressing my doubts and fears, which were evidently shared by the other thirty-five people in the class; then he told us why and how hypnosis works.

The first notes I wrote down were, "Hypnosis is a natural state of mind. The mind and body are inseparable; *if your*

7

mind does not work for you, it will work against you. The three signals when you're out of step with your nature are: pain, unhappiness and frustration. EVERYTHING YOU THINK VIBRATES THROUGH YOUR BODY. What you think of as your 'mind' is composed primarily of two parts, the conscious and the subconscious. By far the smaller of the two, the conscious mind is the thinking, rational part which deals with logical thought and responses to the outer world. The larger subconscious is the feeling, uncritical, obeying part, which operates whether you are awake or asleep. *Its* food is images, and that's what we're going to feed it.''

I was inundated with more information and excited by the possibility that I might be able to change my body responses. If I could lessen my allergies, I would become a believer. It was the perfect test: I had nothing to lose, everything to gain. I'd had severe allergies at intervals in my life; I had often been incapacitated by the sneezing and wheezing, or listless and drugged from antihistamines taken to relieve the symptoms. A year ago, a doctor had told me I was on the verge of bronchial asthma and since then I had been getting allergy shots; they helped, but I didn't like being dependent on them.

During the break, I asked Jim how I could use my mind to eliminate allergies. He surprised me by saying, ''Well, you can't tell yourself you don't have them if you do. Go after it another way.''

I told him about the shots, and he said, ''Each time you hypnotize yourself, visualize—in every minute detail—going to the allergist. SEE yourself getting the shots, but don't actually take them. Practice this twice a day, and you'll see how well it works.''

At the end of the session, he gave us our first instructions in self-hypnosis: ''Loosen your belts, put your feet flat on the floor, shut your eyes and visualize each part of your body, telling it to relax. I'll lead you through it in class; you practice at home. Now, give yourself the suggestion that you'll be wide awake in twenty minutes, feeling wonderful.''

It worked fairly well; I did relax even though the hard chair was quite uncomfortable. It worked much better at home where I was able to lie down, make myself comfortable and feel less self-conscious. Each time I visualized myself driving to the allergist, I wore different clothes and had a current conversation with the nurse. It was so real, I actually winced as I pictured the long, thin needles going in each arm and the redness and swelling that always followed the shots. It was too soon to know whether or not it would work.

I could hardly wait for the second class. Jim said, ''The most important thing to remember is that any idea you hold to be true in your subconscious mind becomes binding upon you and determines the outcome of your behavior. Know that it may NOT be true—your subconscious can't judge that for itself. When you relive an incident or reinforce a condition, you're living in the past. When you change your imagery you can live in the present. So use it to your advantage!''

I was doing dishes three days later when a memory came to me that I hadn't recalled in years. I'd gone on a blind date in high school and immediately discovered that I couldn't stand the boy. He wasn't in any way unpleasant or rude—I just had an intense dislike of him. Within an hour, I had developed an embarrassingly loud, messy sneezing attack and asked to be taken home. I'd laughed about it at the time, but the disturbing thought popped up that perhaps I used allergies to avoid what I didn't want to face, couldn't deal with. That can't be true now, I thought, but the idea persisted no matter how hard I tried to forget it.

Apparently I had an easier time hypnotizing myself than most of the other class members. The only thing that occasionally disturbed me was a buzzing fly in the room, and no matter how much I told myself I didn't hear it, I did. One day, a fly landed on my nose, and as I leaped up to run for the flyswatter, I stubbed my toe on the bedframe and crashed to the floor, aborting any attempt at relaxation for that session.

Generally the room was quiet, my daughters learned not to disturb me when my door was shut, and the usual neighborhood street noises stayed in the background as I pictured each part of my body, told it to relax, and then imagined myself getting shots. Occasionally I had an itchy nose or a twitchy muscle; Jim said to use it, not deny it or I'd become distracted and the self-hypnosis would be impossible. So I said to myself, "The more my cheek itches, the deeper into relaxation I go." It worked! By the third week I automatically came back to full awareness at the end of the practice period, relaxed and calm. I didn't even need to look at the clock any more; my eyes would fly open after twenty minutes and I knew it was time to get back to my household.

By the end of the six-week session I'd had no allergies and no shots. I was impressed. Normally, it was the worst time of the year for me; the desert winds that sporadically blew into Los Angeles in the late summer and early fall had always given me notice before the weatherman knew of them; my runny nose and sneezes would awaken me in the middle of the night. But this year was different, and now I looked forward to hypnotizing myself twice a day as if it were a beneficial tranquilizing drug, one with no undesirable side effects. I was noticeably calmer with the girls and a bit less likely to take irritations to heart. While Larry was not at all interested in the class, he did appreciate the gradual changes in me and said he could tell if I'd skipped a hypnosis session.

Of course I signed up for a more advanced series of classes with Jim. He said, "In order to reprogram your mind, you need three things: relaxation, imagination, and repetition." I was an apt pupil and now found I could get into the hypnotic state very quickly.

In addition to our daily hypnosis, he gave little homework assignments to play with. One of them was called 'automatic writing,' which involved sitting with a pad of paper and pen and letting the subconscious write while the mind let go of any effort to control it. I tried it perhaps half a dozen times with absolutely no results, and I told myself it was, after all, a rather silly exercise.

One night, Larry and I were lying in bed watching the television replay of a Rams football game we'd seen the previous week. I wasn't particularly interested in seeing it again and was sleepy besides. I was resting against a comfortable pillow with the blank pad of paper on my lap, half-dozing and listening to the jazz music that underscored the game. Suddenly my hand began to move in strange, elliptical motions. I made no effort to control or stop it—just stared in fascination as my woman's hand wrote in ungainly childlike scrawls. A flash of memory came in: it looked like the first handwriting exercises I'd ever done—the Palmer Method, they'd called it. Suddenly it stopped. Very slowly and painstakingly my hand wrote

MOMY

I wonder what that means? I thought, and then I knew: it—or I—was misspelling the word MOMMY. But I was such a good speller. I would never make an error on such a simple word.

"Oh, my God, honey, look at this!" I said, and Larry glanced over and then back at the television screen, patting me absent-mindedly on the arm. What I'd written surely didn't look impressive; nonetheless, a little quiver of excitement ran through me. My hand was still writing in large, continuous ellipses despite my strong, unspoken commands to stop. It was very strange, but certainly harmless, I was sure.

At our next class I showed Jim what I'd written. I was the only one in the class who'd done the exercise. He suggested I continue—perhaps the writing might develop further. Excited, I went home to practice. Nothing happened. If I expected to write, I couldn't; if I was just taking a break from a busy day and demanded nothing more than a rest, the writing came. I got annoyed at the unpredictability of the whole thing; I was accustomed to doing things thoroughly, and on time.

One day, weeks later, while sitting quietly and watching my hand scribble away, I thought of asking a question: what do you like best about self-hypnosis?

me like to lie down and rest awhile and lose me tight insides

I could hardly believe the evidence under my hand: something or somebody was writing words that weren't in my mind. Why hadn't I asked questions sooner?

Jim suggested I ask who *was* doing the writing. The next time I put the pad of paper on my lap and asked, my hand wrote, very clearly and distinctly

me melle

Who is Melle? I wrote, unfamiliar with the name.

me be the inside girl here.....me be inside eyes.....
me be big new eyes for seing things

Over the next several months I asked Melle many questions, and once I deciphered her handwriting, her responses invariably surprised me. Melle spelled phonetically, didn't punctuate or capitalize, and never inserted spaces between words. She always wrote in the present tense, and differentiated between 'me' and 'I.'

Melle, what are you most afraid of?

me and i are skeered of being left alone

Why are you afraid of being left alone?

me do be hereing bad stories of it

I finally figured out, after analyzing many pages of her large, childish scrawl, that Melle represented my subconscious, and always responded in the 'here and now.' The 'I' referred to my conscious mind. It was a very separate entity to her. There was no doubt that Melle was an outlet for subconscious thoughts, and as such, it was fun but not extraordinary. It was just that most people never took the time to practice this rather unusual form of dialogue. Even fewer wanted to hear about it.

Except Jim. I typed my questions and Melle's answers I'd written the previous week; often he read it to our class, and occasionally suggested questions to ask her.

One day I asked Melle to write about illness.

the body be singing plain to the hed alla time but
most heds not be listning for the inside music.....
they pretending they not be knowing

What does the body sing?

be singing good things and bad things both.....it be
singing bad things when the foods come out rong or
the body not be moving easy

What else?

good things when the body be warm and easy and touching and humming and singing and dancing by itself

Go on.

the body be telling of the hurts by the WHERE it hurts

Melle, please give me an example.

you be knowing alreddy but me be telling you anyways even if it be stupid

Thanks. Go on.

when the nose be full and the eyes be running and the pains be in the belly and the needuls be in the arms me be telling you that you be not smelling or seing or feeling the way you really be on the inside and you be pretending..... you really be saying to the body that the feeling not be OK to comed out—so the feeling be stopped up like in a bottle and so the running things come out the places it comed out because it not coming out the mouthhole

Go on.

so if a feeling not be coming out the hole it sposed to, it coming out another

Melle was right. I hadn't consciously thought about any emotional situations in such a simplistic manner, yet I did know, now that she spoke in such a visual way, that my allergy problems had resumed and greatly intensified when my husband's parents and mine had stopped speaking to each other. It was extremely painful for me, for Larry and I were both only children and very close to our families. It seemed apparent now that allergies were less connected to pollen than to people.

Jim insisted that our choice of words affected our behavior in subtle ways. We made a verbal 'contract' with him that we would not use the word TRY. He claimed it implied failure, and when we used it, however casually, we were programming ourselves to fail. "If you say, 'I tried to get to class on time,' the unexpressed remainder is 'I tried...and failed.' If you had actually GOTTEN to class on time, you wouldn't have needed to say anything. You would have *done* it. Are you all willing to agree to pay me 25 cents every time you use TRY? Whether you're in class or not?" We laughingly agreed.

The following week we all handed over money. Becoming aware of one simple word hadn't proved to be as easy as we'd thought. It graphically brought home the lesson that we reinforced negativity without even realizing we were doing so.

I had not been aware that I was a negative person, yet in many ways—many hidden ways—I was. I recalled vividly that as a child I had been bitterly disappointed one year at coming down with measles, then mumps, then chickenpox; I hadn't been able to go to camp or begin school on time. I remembered vowing that I would never joyfully anticipate anything again; I thought this would be a less painful way to deal with disappointments in life. I told myself that by pretending I didn't care even if I did, I'd never feel bad when something I wanted very much didn't happen. It felt very adult and much safer to *pretend* to be something on the surface that wasn't true deep inside. By assuming expectations would not be met, I would be surprised and delighted when good things happened, so I reasoned. That would make everything come out even, and I liked being in control of thoughts. It made me feel less vulnerable to hurts, especially those inflicted at school by children who found me very 'different,' and did not appreciate my desire to excel at studies or my lonely pursuits of drawing and writing. But I felt inadequate in dealing with most of my classmates, and avoided painful confrontations when I could by leaving the scene and pretending I didn't feel hurt when pain overwhelmed me. I remembered having frequent allergy attacks that incapacitated me, forcing mother to keep me home from school. Heredity had determined my weakest link, and allergies were my reaction to stress.

I thought of myself as a very enthusiastic, direct, positive person, long over my childhood insecurities, but when I looked into many statements, I saw the negativity, often subtle. It was important to me to look good, and I knew I appeared to be a cheerful, happy woman; underneath, I often doubted myself, and, listening carefully now, I knew my words gave me away and revealed insecurities I hid very well.

In Jim's class I learned that I reinforced negativity with statements such as "I have allergies." I learned to say, "I'm letting go of my allergies." And I was.

Melle helped by being simple and visual. I asked questions about my emotions, feeling foolish in the beginning but amazed and excited at the insights I was gaining.

One day I was angry at my daughters for not doing some assigned chores. When I asked Melle about anger, she told me I was mostly angry at *myself* for not being able to control their actions. It was lack of control that frustrated me, more than the undone chores.

It was a novel path to understanding, and as the months went on, I received surprising answers to many things.

How are you today, Melle?

> *once me herd airs moving and it wasn't a wind so i layd down and went into myself and lerned that things going on that i never payd no eyes to but they there anyways and so i guess i still lerning.....some-times i feeling very full of me and i don't care for nobodies to do nothing but me.....other times i just lissen and other times i petting and loving.....i guess they all be me cause they all feel good but difrunt .....i don't trust pepples that ony show one side cause something hiding they not showing and it usually smelly.....so i don't got to be perfect alla time anymore either and i find out i feels easier in my hed for saying what i feels and now i feels better so what comes outa my mouthhole comes in strat (straight) lines and smells better anyways*

Any more?

> *no.....that be a lot if you wanna sit down and look at it*

Another day I asked: Melle, what's new?

i bin saying big things to pepples and some hereing and some dont but they be truefuls whether pepples lissen or not.....truefuls still sitting in the sun waiting to be picked up

What truthfuls, Melle?

bodies tell heds where they be at if heds dont know it by themselves.....if the bodies got hurts and feel bads then the hed is not lissning to what really be going on in there and the body comed out and sock im in the hed and say hey dummy why you not lissning to how you feels and quit pretending you somebody else!

if pains comed in the tummy then the owner of that body better figure out who they wanna hit back at cause that be making the tummy to hurt.....if the legs hurt they wanna be running away from something.....see it be OK to feel all these things if you be knowing those feelings be there and not be pretending they not there.....see not nice means really pretending to be one way but really being another so the feets and the hed and the body not going in the same directions and then nobodies know who is what .....see every part of the body telling things alla time ony kids lissen harder.....and music comed from insides the body too

Melle was becoming very talkative and relished covering pages of newsprint in her large handwriting. I could hardly manage to write fast enough. Words just appeared under my pen without my brain forming any preconceived ideas or images. Melle continued:

it be veryveryvery and more very goods to be silly .....some pepples think silly is dum but ony smart pepples who got heds and feets going in same direction can be silly.....and that means smart cause they be having fun and they be looking at everything with big new eyes like little animal just borned—and colors are bright and air is light and it takes real pepples to see and feel and touch.....and i do be knowing that the scaredy cats rund away cause they looking for black holes to fall into.....and they will find them cause they be looking.....see pepples get what they looking for mostly and i knowed that if somebody sees uglies in everything they gonna be ugly themselves for not seing nothing else.....and there eyes get all squinty and mean and they not nice in any way at all

Melle continued:

if pepples looking for pretties and if a rainy day comed along even the rain be OK cause they needs a little bit for growing too.....but they reddy for sunshine mostly and mostly they find frens to play with cause that makes 'em feel good.....see some pepples is mean cause they socking pepples in the nose before they get it done to them but they ends up with a big fat nose that ony smells icky things and nothing else .....they don't know what they smelling is them sitting in a tight chair holding on with bony fingers cause they thinks some bodies is gonna tip em over

The class and Jim were thoroughly fascinated with Melle. I could not imagine having been the kind of child she was; I'd been more introverted and serious, and certainly not as silly.

I loved her.

Psychic

Jim and the people in my class occasionally wanted Melle to answer questions about their lives. She was usually amazingly accurate, telling of things I didn't know.

I wrestled with the idea that when Melle was correct, it meant I must be psychic. It seemed a strange talent, one that often felt uncomfortable, for there was no safe, sure ground. I was suspicious of my writings for others, because I'd had excellent recall when in school and often was able to write facts I didn't consciously remember. It had stood me in good stead in achieving excellent grades, but now I felt it was possible I was unwittingly cheating; perhaps I'd overheard a shred of conversation which I unknowingly stored and then presented in Melle's style.

She considered the past, present and future as one, and I was often uncertain if what she wrote had happened or was yet to come. Time was described as "dead-leaf time, new-leaf time, green-leaf time and falling-leaf time"—obviously the seasons—but in an unspecified year.

One day I wrote: Melle, please explain how you can write things that you have no way of knowing. Are they right?

18

there aren't no walls like you thinks

What kind of walls?

walls of times and places.....i don't know how it works, but it do—even the little bits that comed to me are from new ears that here difrunt songs than they used to.....see everything in the body makes sounds if you can here it.....i can here sometimes if i cares to

What is time, then?

time be not days and nights and sun and moon..time be vibrashuns between things and pepples.....mens just finding waves make noises, but pepples make noises even when they not saying nothings and sounds comed in colors that the ears here, not the eyes see.....fishes in the sea know things this way, and pepples used to could but now they not lissning

My family was not particularly interested in the automatic writing. Linda, 15, was immersed in a teen world that, naturally enough, didn't include mom's new pastime. It was only when her friends thought it was 'weird' or 'neat' that she occasionally wanted to hear what I wrote. Denise (Denny), 12, promptly left the room if any prolonged discussion of my fascinating new class and writing came up. Larry enjoyed the calming effects of the self-hypnosis on my disposition, but Melle's wit and wisdom escaped him, and I found his lack of interest disappointing; it was basically only my classmates and Jim who encouraged me to continue.

In all fairness, I really couldn't blame Larry. He was always consumed with business or rushing off to play golf, and managed his life with an ease and a constant, cheerful disposition that I envied. I seemed—by comparison—moody, more easily upset by trivial family problems, and quick to flash when the fighting and nit-picking between Linda and Denny reached my saturation point. Larry never expressed anger in any situation, and was the fulcrum in the pendulum of my life. I compared everyone to him: he seemed perfectly wonderful, and the rest of us, exasperatingly human.

I began to confide in a few people outside of class that I had a childlike part of me that wrote interesting things, and friends began to ask if Melle would write for them. Again, as in class, she was correct most of the time, especially when she spoke of events that had happened in their childhood.

What had started as an exercise and developed into a method of self-knowledge was fast becoming a game, a test, and one I wanted to excel at. Although I kept telling myself it didn't matter if I was correct, I didn't want to look at the fact that it was indeed another way for me to measure myself and not be found wanting. Of all the patterns in my life that kept repeating, the one I most avoided seeing was that I had a *need* to be right. It trailed like a shadow, hiding on the cloudy days, and only popping into view when I could see myself clearly, in the sunshine of acceptance.

Once in a while, someone who would ask me to write for her seemed to be a blank page on which I could discern nothing. I didn't know why this happened, and my curiosity was aroused. Why would one person present an invisible barrier and another, an open book? Or was the difference in me, in my interaction with the subject? I always made an effort to relax and center before I began, to let go of all conscious thoughts and accept whatever might come through from my subconscious.

It was a mystery that provoked my first visit to a psychic. I decided to call a woman who I'd heard had exceptional psychic ability; I would give nothing away by anything I said. I'd see what SHE did.

When I called to make the appointment I expected to hear a mysterious foreigner. A cheery voice with a mid-western twang said, "Hello, Louise speaking."

"My name is Bobbie. I'd like an appointment with you." I was careful not to mention my last name, or the name of the woman who'd told me of her.

"How about eleven tomorrow morning?" she responded, and I agreed, wondering why she wasn't busier, but delighted that I wouldn't have to wait any longer.

The next day I dressed carefully and anonymously in faded jeans, a nondescript blue shirt, old tennis shoes and no jewelry except for my thin, unadorned wedding band. I brushed my long hair back into a pony tail and tied it with a scarf. I was glad I drove a Ford—as someone said, the car that couldn't offend anyone—or pigeonhole me either, I thought. On the thirty-five minute drive to Louise's home, I was exhilarated and thought how full my world was of things to do and explore.

Later, I would deliver photo proofs to Jim—an exciting first attempt at triple exposures in each film frame, all shot against a black seamless background: a photographic essay of multiple aspects of a personality. I locked them in the trunk.

I arrived at the pretty white house, surprised to find horses in the clean stable area behind the tree-shaded home. There was evidence of a child as well. I did as Louise had requested and let myself in the back door and waited in the den. It was simple, but clean and attractive. I wondered if she'd seen me driving up, but Louise evidently was with someone else, for I heard a door slam before she came to greet me with a country-girl charm and openness that did not fit my preconceptions of what a psychic should be. She led me to her tiny pink and white bedroom that had ruffled curtains at the windows and portraits of her family on the bureau. She motioned me to sit down at the card table and brought out a pack of well-worn cards. "Cut them three times," she instructed.

It seemed a random method to arrive at information; surely chance was the only factor that operated. But I resolved to monitor my body language and speech so as to reveal nothing. I wanted to test her, trap her. She immediately began speaking of her celebrity clients, including Marilyn Monroe and a world-famous religious figure. If she's good, I thought, why does she have to try to impress me with name-dropping? It seemed a most inauspicious beginning.

She laid the cards in rows and began talking immediately. "Oh, you're a writer," she said first, with some surprise. She didn't look at me or, apparently, expect answers, and continued in a rapid-fire monologue that fit my life very neatly.

"Your husband has had difficult financial times but is approaching more security. He will begin a new business venture in the spring that will bring him financial rewards;

he's excited about this project for the challenge of it. Everyone loves him, and he has a healing influence on people. You have a warm, loving marriage. You have two children." She didn't know whether they were girls or boys.

I was definitely enthralled, although among the truths she threw in many unknowns: "You will have an extremely long life, and will have three marriage ceremonies, two to the same man. There will not be a divorce. You will outlive him and marry again, although he will live a long time also." I felt briefly threatened and wished she hadn't said anything about a future without Larry, no matter how far away it was.

Louise scooped up the cards, took out a ouija board and asked me to prepare questions while she was contacting her 'spirit guides.' She didn't explain what that was, but I was covertly fascinated, and reached down to touch the plastic indicator that rested on the board.

"Please don't," Louise said abruptly, "I'm the only one who uses it." The indicator began moving rapidly, but she spoke far more quickly than words could be spelled.

She looked at me sharply. "Oh, I see you're a photographer, too!" She seemed very surprised and said, "It's very important that you continue to take pictures with the black sides." I was utterly amazed—how could she know about the pictures locked in my trunk?

The ouija board indicator continued its swift, jerky flight around the board. "Your mother has trouble with words and thoughts." True. But along with more facts, she threw in, "You were in a place with tall white columns, and you danced in a gown of white with gold trim, and were very, very happy."

I asked, "Was it the Acropolis?" for I'd been there and felt I had returned to a long-forgotten home even though I didn't believe in reincarnation. I immediately wished I hadn't given her a hook to hang her next statement on, for she began to talk of other past lives she assured me I'd had. I wanted her to talk about *this* life.

"Tell me about Melle," I asked, to change her focus.

"She's your spirit. She has been ill and is just regaining her vitality. She is of utmost importance." Whenever there was a lapse in the wild movement on the board she said, "Ask. Ask."

I wasn't prepared. All the questions of my life had vanished in this simple farmhouse with a country psychic.

She rambled on, mingling predictions, past lives and show-biz anecdotes with happy abandon until the indicator stopped abruptly and she looked up and said, "That's all."

The session had been about forty-five minutes. I put my $20 bill on the table, thanked her, and left before she could begin another celebrity story. I wouldn't tell Larry what it cost, but I knew I'd never be able to keep my first visit to a psychic to myself, even if he made fun of it.

I was exhilarated but confused, wanting to write down everything before I forgot it.

At lunch, by myself, I vacillated between an urge to defend Louise and the need to discount much of what she'd said. I took a sheet of paper and divided it into four sections, categorizing everything I could remember into:

1) Future. UNPROVABLE. WORTHLESS. How would I know I'd live a long and happy life until I'd lived it? On the other hand, for short-term predictions I knew I was suggestible. Once an idea was planted, it grew, as I knew through self-hypnosis. She was positive rather than negative, so that was a plus.

2) Generalized information based on probabilities or shrewd assessments of age, race, appearance. DISCOUNT THIS INFORMATION. "You have two children, but I feel a third is like your child." I thought I remembered the statistical average was 2.3 children per family, and her statement was a good hedge, although it was also quite true. I probably looked contented, so she could assume a happy marriage.

3) Specific information. AMAZING! No one had ever guessed I was a photographer, and she even picked up the detail of an unusual job. She'd said I primarily took pictures of nature rather than people, plus other accurate fragments, improbable to have guessed.

4) Reincarnation statements. PURE JUNK! I felt strangely ambivalent about the session, both excited by her accuracy and dissatisfied with the number of unprovable statements. I wished she hadn't spoken so quickly, so glibly; she didn't seem to need to search for information, doubt that it was true, or need a response.

I wondered what people really thought of me after I'd written for them. I oozed uncertainty and constantly wanted corroboration that I was accurate. Even friends who had praised my insights had sometimes asked, "Do you *really* read people's minds?" I'd had to reassure them, telling the truth: "No, not at all. I don't know what's in your mind, and don't want to know. The information seems to come from some level I can't explain. Words just appear on the paper, often without any connection to thoughts or images." At least I didn't charge anything. I couldn't imagine a tougher profession than being a professional psychic.

I couldn't wait to call the friend who'd recommended Louise. I wanted to make sure she hadn't talked to the psychic and inadvertently slipped in a few revealing facts about me.

She hadn't spoken to her in months.

ESP

Larry and I went away with another couple, Anne and Pete Moran; they were new friends with whom we played bridge, and we were a compatible foursome who decided ten days in Colorado would provide time for cards, golf for the men, and photography opportunities for me. After several days in Denver and a breathtaking ride over the continental divide, we unpacked our clothes in a small apartment in Dillon that overlooked the mountains, and prepared to spend a quiet few days luxuriating in the time to play bridge after breakfast, lunch and dinner, interrupted only for food and sleep.

Anne and Pete thought my ventures into the paranormal were amusing and I had promised to do some of my 'funny writing' for them when I was in the mood. One night after some wine and before dinner, I was.

My hand began writing names, which Anne confirmed were those of her childhood best friends in Philadelphia. I felt relaxed, and under no pressure to prove anything. I told her I'd like to ramble on before she asked any questions.

I described a dress which Anne said was a perfect picture of her wedding suit twenty-eight years before. Suddenly the handwriting changed and I wrote:

bebe annie broked it.....broked it and the momy mad

Well, I thought, all children break things. That doesn't sound like much to go on. But my hand continued to struggle for a word to complete a picture of a doll which Anne had broken.

the doll be made of.....

and my hand wrote words I couldn't decipher. Sounds came out of me I wasn't able to interpret: one sounded like 'biscuit.' I couldn't go to another subject, for my hand had stopped writing and would not move.

"I've got it!" Anne said with a big grin. "I was a very young child when my mother gave me a family heirloom to play with—a bisque doll. I broke it. It couldn't be fixed, and my mother was heartbroken. Funny thing—she just mentioned it last week, and this happened more than forty years ago."

"What's bisque?"

"It's china or porcelain. They used to handpaint the face. I've seen others, but never as beautiful."

"Well, I'm glad that's cleared up so we can move along." I smiled, and thought it was one of the most trivial bits Melle had ever picked up. Dolls had never been important to me.

I drank some more wine, looked at the mountains changing colors in the twilight, and the words flowed on:

your fren thinks she died and she be skeered.....
your fren looked in the mirror and thinks she died

The silence between us seemed dense, as though I had encroached on private territory that was not mine to invade. I never wanted to write in order to pry, only to illuminate or amuse.

"That must be wrong," I said lamely.

"No, it's right," she said at last. "No one knows the story behind what you wrote except Pete and me. My best friend had a twin sister who was killed in a car crash. They were identical twins, and every time my friend looked in the mirror, she saw her dead sister's face. She had a rough time of it emotionally for a while; I thought she was going to have a nervous breakdown, and I tried to help her in every way I could. Finally I came up with a silly idea, but one that helped: I told her to dye her hair a different color and change her makeup. Amazing that you could pick that up about my friend; I've never told anyone, and we don't discuss it anymore, either.''

It was getting chilly, so we moved indoors. It was Anne's turn to fix dinner; I asked Pete if he wanted me to write for him, wondering if his skepticism about psychic phenomena would deter my writing. We decided we'd have more privacy in the bedroom. I sat on the bed near the only lamp, Pete on the floor against a closet door, face shadowed.

The writing immediately took on an ominous tone. I couldn't write fast enough to express the feelings galloping through me. I spoke rapidly, adding to the words, seeing a picture form as though a movie screen had appeared on the wall. I saw pins in a map being changed, men floundering in water, and Pete in the grip of pure terror. He was a man in a black abyss of fear. Another scene: more danger, a man's name written—all of it a mystery as I talked nonstop and began suddenly, inexplicably, to cry, feeling myself overwhelmed by the knowledge of a death he'd barely escaped.

''Yes. All of it's true,'' he said in a strange voice, obviously gripped by the despair of an old scene revived. ''I was in the Merchant Marines. At the last moment our ship was transferred out of a convoy; every ship in that convoy was sunk—and many buddies of mine died. I escaped the war unhurt, but some time later I did have a near-fatal accident in which I was nearly crushed between a ship and a wall. You gave the name of the friend who saved me.''

I'd known nothing of what my hand had written, but I didn't feel like crowing; I was shaking, and needed to get away from the overpowering sensation that I'd just peered into a life full of pain and had unintentionally permitted it to enter me. I wanted dinner and our usual light evening.

I didn't choose to write again and we passed the rest of the trip lightly.

* * *

The allergies were completely gone, and I no longer needed to visualize getting shots. It was easy to hypnotize myself and relax, and my subconscious seemed freer to come up with unexpected imagery that occasionally proved prophetic.

One afternoon I lay down intending to relax the tension I felt coming on. I'd shown my portfolio of photographs to an editor of the corporate newspaper at Atlantic Richfield; he'd given me an assignment to shoot an event which they were co-sponsoring, an all-Asian get-together in a park. Thousands of people were expected and they wanted human interest shots, complete with names of every person in any picture they might print. I was thrilled they liked my work, but worried as well, for other than photos of my children I rarely did any candid photography; still, it was too much of a plum to turn down and would certainly be a learning experience. Denny agreed to be my assistant and record names as I called out the film frame, so that would be a big help.

As I slipped gently into a relaxed state, I had a vision of a ladder. I couldn't dismiss the image and felt it was somehow important to take when I shot the job. When I got up after twenty minutes and began to load the car for the next day's shooting, I thought, what the hell—I've got plenty of room. I'm sure it won't be necessary, but it can't hurt to pack it.

The next day, just before the big drawing in which Arco was giving the main prize, one of their men mentioned that the publicity banners over the Arco booth were down. "This is the shot we really need," he groaned. "I'd give anything for a ladder but nobody here has one, not even the maintenance people."

"I've got one," I said casually, and mentally applauded my subconscious, resolving to pay more attention to what I'd assumed was idle mind chatter and imagery.

It was another step in listening to an inner wisdom that apparently knew the future and could help me prepare for it.

I couldn't recall ever being psychic. If the ability had been there, why would it appear now? I had learned through experience—despite my skepticism—that self-hypnosis liberated the subconscious, and that must be where the abilities were. Melle's writings, the occasional intuitive and psychic occurrences, and the disappearance of allergies must be linked. I couldn't see a logical connection, yet it was the only explanation that made any sense.

I felt like a child with a magic carpet—I could fly in ways I'd never dreamed were possible!

Touch

I persuaded some of my friends to take Jim's course in self-hypnosis. All enjoyed it, some used it, but most just practiced the relaxation techniques for a while, then stopped. Life was too busy, they said, to take the time.

Larry and I took Jim's class together. I found it amazing that I'd missed so many details the first time, and enjoyed it as much, if not more, the second time around. There was so very much to learn! It was wonderful sharing my enthusiasm with Larry, who was fascinated, suspicious and intrigued, and invariably fell asleep during the self-hypnosis practice period. An ability to sleep instantly whenever he needed a little rest had always been one of his greatest gifts; now it worked against him.

My good friend, Elynore (Ely) Leigh, also agreed to study with Jim. I once believed she had peculiar ideas; her interest in extra-sensory phenomena had always repulsed me, but now I found myself involved with the very things I'd once condemned, no longer considering them objectionable when my own experiences validated the information. I couldn't deny what I knew had happened.

Jim had told me about a woman who gave him acupressure treatments which he claimed helped revitalize and 'balance' him. It sounded interesting, so I signed up for Barbra Rapko's acupressure class. My friend Beth had been very ill and she decided to go too. I practiced on her at the first session, and watched in amazement as my fumbling hands brought her relaxation and pain relief. Barbra had to touch her to bring her out of a deep, placid state so she'd be alert enough to drive home. I was sure I hadn't done anything special, yet some change, however temporary, had occurred. I couldn't explain it, but once again—with great eagerness—I began to explore a new field that contradicted everything I'd been brought up to believe was true: that medicine held all the answers.

In the class, we practiced upon one another. Barbra made a statement which apparently sank in more deeply than I could have believed possible. "When you don't know what to do," she said, "*TRUST YOURSELF TO KNOW WHAT TO DO.*" They proved to be some of the most significant words I would ever hear.

I signed up for an advanced acupressure class although I had no intention of becoming a professional as did some of the others. I just felt it would be very handy, and I was interested in the vast storehouse of oriental knowledge that was at the core of the class.

Barbra explained that the Chinese concept of life differs sharply from Western beliefs. The yin/yang symbolizes the idea of life as movement between opposite poles. Nothing, no one is ever frozen into an unchanging reality; therefore, everything has its peaks and valleys, its ups and downs. One could not *have* an 'up' without its counterpart, as light has no comparison without knowledge of dark. Wholeness, wellness, always encompasses both polarities, and the Chinese have always seen pain, or any symptom, as revealing an aspect of the total body; rather than only treating the symptom, they examine the life of the person to understand why the symptom is manifesting. Body, mind and spirit all unite to keep an individual balanced. In China, doctors were paid when their patients were well, not ill. Therefore, they had both a financial and professional interest in keeping patients healthy.

I loved the inquisitive minds and gentle hands of my class members. We practiced on one another, adding bits and pieces of helpful, non-medical treatments from our own experiences. One woman said she'd suffered from violent migraines all her life, until she'd been told to take four or five digestive enzyme tablets at the very first twinge of an approaching migraine. She'd not had a headache since.

My mother, too, suffered from similar headaches, obviously the result of stress and her body's tendency toward that expression of incapacitation, just as mine had been severe allergies. She no longer had them, so I couldn't judge the effectiveness of the tablets. I did remember, however, that as a child I had stood in the doorway of her bedroom, watching her writhe in pain and violently sick from the medication; something in me made a vow that I would never, ever have headaches. I rarely did.

Instead, I seemed to have an aptitude to heal others of their headaches without knowing precisely what I was doing. The relaxation techniques allowed me to calm and center myself, acupressure taught me that healing was possible without medicine, and my newborn intuition guided my hands in movements that brought relief to others.

I felt an inner exultation that I was sometimes able to transform pain into wellness. The process, whether it was the changing awareness within me or an actual healing on others, was so beneficial I felt like Dorothy in the *Wizard of Oz* following the yellow brick road. And, like a child, I thought I would always be able to pick and choose what I would change and never have any growing pains.

Hands

In class, Barbra mentioned that a woman she greatly admired was giving a one-day workshop we might wish to attend. The woman, Dr. Dolores Krieger, was a nurse and an Associate Professor at New York University where she had given the first class of its kind in the United States fully accredited towards a master's degree: therapeutic human touch as a healing force. The one-day class would be a very brief summary of what she taught on a semester basis to nurses going for a Master's or Ph.D. degree.

I signed up to go with a friend. The class met in the basement meeting room of the Church of Religious Science with about twenty people attending.

Dee Krieger was a stocky, unadorned woman who was direct and humorous in her approach to her work. "They call my students 'Krieger's Krazies,'" she began, "but I'm telling you that we all have a natural potential to use therapeutic touch. I'll give you some background, we'll do a few exercises to demonstrate what can be done, and then we'll practice on each other. You'll be amazed how comfortable you'll be with it by the end of the day.

"In this scientific age, we've all but forgotten that every culture has had its practitioners of the laying-on of hands to help or to heal. The healer transfers energy to the healee, who feels relaxed and may become pain-free from this energy exchange. In the Eastern cultures, a great deal of study has been given this process, and the Chinese have named this energy subsystem CHI. A healthy person has an abundance of it—an ill person, a lack. Not only can this energy be transferred from one person to another, it can be DIRECTED. I believe, moreover, that it is actually the patient who heals himself; the healer merely accelerates the process by directing this CHI."

Dee strode back and forth across the room, vibrating with energy and enthusiasm. It was contagious, and when she was finished, I could hardly wait to actually practice what she preached. "Sit comfortably in your chair, feet flat on the floor, elbows away from the trunk of your body, arms not resting on your lap. Now bring your palms close together without touching, fingers pointing up. Shut your eyes if you wish, and direct yourself to sense into the space between your hands. When you become aware of a sensation—any sensation—separate your palms by about two inches, then slowly bring them back to the original position, about one-quarter inch apart."

I felt as though there was a ball of some sort in the empty space, and that I was actually compressing something tangible when I brought my hands back together. We repeated the movement several times, extending our range to four, six, then eight inches, always bringing the hands back to the original position. My palms tingled pleasantly when my hands neared each other and I was aware that the field between them had warmth and something else I couldn't define. It wasn't quite palpable, nor visual, but it was there.

Dee said, "This exercise will demonstrate that *you do not stop at your skin*. When you practice, you'll notice how sensitive you become to the field around the healee's body. Clothing makes no difference; the energy field penetrates it very easily and information will make itself known to you that you'll use as a base from which to direct your energies."

We took a short break. When we reassembled, Dee asked us to arrange our chairs in a tight circle. "Put a pad of paper and a pencil in your lap," she instructed. "Close your eyes if you wish. Knowing that you don't stop at your skin, become aware of your right shoulder and the space just beyond it. See if you can sense into the space just as you did the field between your hands. Now, extend the aware space until it reaches toward your right-hand neighbor. Don't move or make any effort. If any visual impressions pop into your mind, tell yourself to keep them in your memory until you write them down. Just allow whatever comes to mind to remain there, without judging the content."

The woman next to me was a stranger. As I concentrated on her, impressions came flooding in swiftly; a white picket fence, a blue bicycle which had been involved in an accident, and many other details of a life dissimilar to mine. It was a bit like painting by number, making certain connections without knowing what the entire picture would look like. When Dee called time, we all wrote on our papers, then compared notes to find out if we'd been accurate. Everything I'd written had been in the woman's life, but they'd all been fleeting images of scenes, and trivial ones at that. It felt like automatic writing had at first—simple, child-like images—and I realized I was quite comfortable knowing something without knowing HOW I knew it.

I was having a grand time, absorbing everything Dee said as though I were a book with blank pages waiting to be filled. It was all much easier than going to school and learning by rote. I'd loved school—mostly—but this hands-on learning felt utterly natural.

Later in the afternoon, after stories of Dee's fascinating experiences, questions from us, and more exercises, we separated into groups of four or five.

"Select one person to lie down on a table, one to take notes, and the other two or three to take turns scanning the 'patient,'" she instructed. "Very slowly, beginning at the head, bring both hands down the subject's body, and be aware of anything the energy field tells you. You may get heat, cold, tingling, whatever. As you move down the subject's body without touching it, describe what you sense to the person recording. When you're through, your 'patient' can tell you if you were accurate. Take turns, so you may have all the experiences.''

I was a scanner before I was a patient. As I moved my hands in the air over an unknown person, I felt funny 'bumps,' cold and hot spots, as though I were swimming in water that had variable temperature patterns flowing through it. I wasn't familiar enough with anatomy to know where all the organs were located, but I unmistakably sensed that the air around her was charged with differences. When we reviewed my comments, she said I'd been accurate as far as I'd spoken. I had missed some ailments, but had discovered an arthritic knee and an old surgery scar hidden by her clothes.

Not bad, I thought. Not bad for a beginning.

When it was my turn to lie on the table to be scanned by each of the others, I realized I didn't have many physical problems. No one was able to pick up that I'd had polio in my left leg although the calf muscle was still slightly smaller than the right. One woman noticed a change in the energy field over my right ankle, where I'd fallen and chipped a bone the year before.

The class was concluded shortly after the scanning exercise. It had been a full day, but for me had ended much too soon.

Larry and I joined some friends for dinner in a restaurant that evening. I showed everyone the hand exercises I had learned. I was amazed that even in a crowded room, despite the commotion all around me, I still seemed quite sensitive to the energy field. I decided to practice every day, if only for a few minutes. As with self-hypnosis, only good could result. I had nothing to lose, everything to learn.

Bursitis

Larry came home with a painful left elbow after playing golf one Saturday. The pain intensified until his left arm was virtually useless. The slightest pressure was agony. Even though he used his right hand for nearly everything, he could not bear the weight of his left arm just resting on a table. The very worst part, in his opinion, was the disruption to his golf swing.

He made an appointment with a doctor, something he normally postponed as long as possible. The orthopedic surgeon confirmed what Larry had suspected: an acute case of bursitis. The doctor shot the arm with cortisone. It helped—for a day. The pain returned with full force, and Larry went back for another shot, then a third. The surgeon suggested the possibility of surgery if the elbow didn't improve. Larry's dislike of surgery was not nearly as intense as his fear of missing golf for several months if he had the operation.

As we got into bed one night, he said, "Honey, is there anything you can do? The cortisone is wearing off already."

I knew I was the last resort, for Larry didn't believe in the healing practices I was learning. Acupressure and the laying on of hands had no place in his life; they were strictly *my* interests.

"Well, I guess I can't hurt you," I replied, with a distinct lack of confidence. I knew that bursitis is an inflammation of a sac around a joint—I'd looked it up in the dictionary.

What am I going to do? I thought. What the hell can I do with a sore elbow? I considered not doing anything. I rarely treated anyone with anything worse than a headache. But why take courses in healing if I didn't give it a chance? Barbra's words came back: "If you don't know what to do, trust yourself to know." That certainly seemed appropriate now. I decided to take a chance and trust.

Larry was lying on his right side waiting for me to begin. I lay next to him on the bed, staring at his back and elbow.

"Honey, take some deep, slow breaths. Acknowledge that you have the pain, and give yourself permission to let it go."

"Do I have to believe this stuff?" he asked.

"No, but it couldn't hurt! If you don't believe that healing is possible, just be neutral. Don't set up a wall against it, OK? Let whatever happens, happen."

"OK," he murmured. Any time he was horizontal, sleep was just a blink away.

I laid my left hand as gently as possible on his elbow. I could feel the heat radiating from it. The joint was far hotter than the rest of his arm. When I treated headaches, I always felt cold emanating from the pain point. What should I do with heat?

I changed my position, got more comfortable, closed my eyes and took several slow, deep breaths.

My hand on his elbow didn't give me the sense that I was doing anything helpful. I felt a strong urge to lay my hand across the back of his neck; I cupped my right hand around the base of his skull and held it there firmly. I noticed that I was breathing more slowly, reaching to hear an inner voice that would guide me. I didn't hear a voice, but information seemed to present itself to me in some way that was neither aural nor visual. My hands moved of their own volition, as though I had little control. My left hand rested on his wrist, then on his inner elbow, then his biceps muscle. The feeling became stronger that the pain was really coming from his neck, particularly from the right side, just at the hair line. I'd learned in my studies that "have to," "must" and "should" commands came through that pathway, that side—one reason for stiff necks, expressive of hidden resentment at having to do what one does not want to do. I was certain that traditional medicine would dismiss all this as nonsense, so it was an opportunity to test what I had learned.

I'm intellectualizing, I thought. I'll just let my hands go where they choose.

My right hand refused to go anywhere and stayed warmly curved on his neck. I was tiring quickly, my feet were falling asleep, and I wondered if I had the energy to sustain any effort much longer. I brought my left hand back to Larry's elbow and circled above it, about an inch from his skin. I held the palm flat, fingers together, and shook it after every few circling motions, as though I was shaking off water.

I was about to question Larry to see if I had relieved any pain when I heard his peaceful snore. I covered him, turned out the lights and quickly fell asleep.

The next morning, I heard a surprised "hummphh" as he stretched and sat up.

"What?" I muttered, not yet awake.

"My elbow is better, honey. It really is! I can clench my hand without pain shooting through my arm as it has for the past month. It hurts, but nothing like it did. Will you do your hocus-pocus again tonight?"

"Sure. I'm so glad you're feeling better." I was as surprised as he was.

For the next ten nights, I went through the motions of laying on hands as though I knew what I was doing. Sometimes I felt no heat when he said the joint was tender; other times I felt heat when he felt little or no pain. His distress lessened from the original acute stage to soreness to slight tenderness to...nothing. After two weeks, he was playing golf as though he'd never heard of bursitis.

I benefited as much as he did. I felt a new sense of confidence in my abilities. I wanted to study more, learn more, practice more.

Larry's attitude toward my studies changed dramatically, and he loved to tell the story of his recovery, glorifying my "hocus-pocus."

But, like all golden coins, this experience had two sides. The satisfaction from Larry's relating the story shriveled under questions. "What did you REALLY do?" "How does that stuff work?" "Can anybody do it?" All were unanswerable questions, at least by me.

When I most expected results from the laying-on of hands, nothing happened. I had a magic touch with headaches, but everything else was unpredictable. I treated friends' ailments, and some I helped...temporarily. I wondered if the touch of loving, unschooled hands would have done as well. I didn't know where the benefits of acupressure ended and just plain caring began. Healing was obviously possible. But who did it? Did I? Did the 'patient' set some force in motion when verbal permission to get well was offered? Why were some results lasting, as with Larry, and others not? I'd never worked with victims of strokes, cancer or other major traumas to the body —could they be helped, their downward spirals changed?

The healing path was a powerful ego potion and the taste of my new-found "power" was highly intoxicating. Only the unpredictability of results saved me from becoming really obnoxious. I learned not to make claims I might not be able to substantiate.

And most of all, deepest of all, was the profound sense that the power to heal, to make well, to make whole, was but a part of a much larger dimension. I cautiously avoided confronting the idea of God, of Source, so that I could remain a comfortable agnostic, an unchallenged doubter. But where WAS the boundary between honest doubt that led onward to intelligent investigation; and disbelief, which subverted energy and did not support an unprejudiced commitment to learn?

Light

I was in a deep sleep one night when an extraordinary thing happened.

A startling blue light awoke me. At first I thought I was dreaming, and moved to rub my eyes and sit up to make sure I was awake.

The light intensified. I marveled at the exquisite color, so much richer than any blue I'd ever seen. I wanted to hold it, wrap myself in it, let it be mine forever.

I had no sooner passed from wonder to possession than it began to change to an intense, radiant white. The rational me was afraid I'd be blinded by its power, as though I were inside a mushroom cloud, but I could not shut my eyes, mesmerized by the incandescence.

My eyes were unaccustomed to such brilliance. I wondered if this was a 'vision,' but I saw only shimmering light, not forms or substance, and the thought disappeared like a mirage.

I had no sooner reconciled myself to observing this singular universe than it disappeared. I half expected to find some residue of light in the room, but all was as it had been.

I felt altered by an invisible hand, as though I had been momentarily allowed to see another dimension. The feeling stayed behind, like radioactive fallout, that something had changed and would never be the same.

At a deeper level, I felt it signified a healing of some kind, but of what, I didn't know. I had not been ill.

Paul

Melle was a fact of my life, but I wrote very sporadically. Sometimes weeks—even months—went by without my feeling a need to write; occasionally I would write every day for a week. When my life was flowing smoothly, I didn't question it; when pressure built up, I got out the newsprint pad, centered myself, and posed questions.

I assumed that Melle would always be there when I asked, but about four years after she first began to write, a puzzling change occurred.

After the appearance of the Light, a new voice came through my writing—one which had a very different perspective. An unfamiliar rhythm and strangely spiritual words appeared on paper. I was embarrassed and unwilling to talk about the change, for I didn't want to be branded as an "eccentric." I wasn't aware of any inner changes that could account for the new and different voice.

I was unwilling to show the writing to those who expected Melle's basic humor. In my avoidance of exposing this new voice, I neglected to ask "Who are you?"

I confided in Barbra, who suggested I find out who *was* answering.

My hand wrote the word

Paul

Oh—a male voice, I thought. How peculiar. I let further interrogation drop until Barbra mentioned it might be interesting to find out if Paul had a last name.

Paul of Tarsus

my hand wrote. The name sounded familiar, but I couldn't quite place it.

Barbra was shocked and delighted. "You mean you've never heard of St. Paul, the great Theologian of the Church?" she asked.

"Is that Paul of Tarsus?"

"Yes," she said. "He was a Jew—Saul, later to become Paul. Haven't you ever heard of his writings?"

"No. Not that I recall. Of course I've heard the name of St. Paul, but I don't remember anything about him. I can't believe this whole thing. Maybe it'll go away."

But it didn't go away.

Melle no longer appeared; only Paul answered in her place. The answers were upsetting in their religiosity and intimations that I had a book to write and changes to make.

In July, 1975 I wrote: Melle, will you write for me?

I am Paul. Ask.

Tell me about my mental set now.

Waiting.

For what?

Trust.

Why is that? Please explain.

Necessary. You will be called. You have come a long way, but are not ready yet. You are in a dark building now with a dim light and you are not yet trusting enough of yourself.

When you no longer need to state what you do, how well you do it, and prove you are alive you will be trusting. Listen, and you will hear.

Why do I have the power of writing things I cannot know or do not believe?

I give . . . . . others give.

For what purpose?

For seeing and transmitting and writing a book—not soon, but preparing . . . . . . hearing sounds not heard by others and feeling with finger vibrations.

Judge not. Trust. All is here but you are not yet ready. Set aside a quiet time each day to listen.

I was less ready to accept this than Melle's easy humor. I stuffed the pages in the back of a drawer.

One night, I was sitting quietly in the den with my eyes shut, resting after a busy day. The television news was on and I was enjoying the brief hour before I had to get dinner on the table. My hand began to write and didn't stop until it had completed many pages.

In the beginning it was said that all who gathered would be free, but that became untrue, because the people gathered rocks and threw them at each other. The people took the ideas that were given to them and used them to cause death and hurtful wounds.

And in the interim those who saw the Light said, "we must change our ways," but the people pretended to listen and did not do the entries in the ledger. The wise men said, "if you will not listen, a great pestilence will be visited upon you," and it was so. But the people did not listen, for the singing in their bones told them they were immortal no matter what they did, so they did not care to change.

And those who had the word—and they were not many—took the burdens on their shoulders and knew the path and knew that few would follow. They waited for a force that would move people to reclaim the deeds of darkness, and they waited in vain. And the leaders of the people were often the strong, but rarely the kind who did move to do good and rid the land of disease and poorness and hunger and unnecessary pains.

One day the sun did not rise and the earth shook equally with great force in all the world: in the deserts and the mountains and the seashores the land shook and the water advanced, or the water poured forth where there was no channel and did fill the land, and the people hid beneath the trees and were smothered in the green branches, and they hid beneath the ground, and the earth opened and closed over them, and they did find no hiding place, for there was none. Few were left, for the earth raged and the sea boiled, and the heavens let down in force what had been stored, and it was more pestilence accumulated.

Those who did abide on the land without fear did know no surprise and were not harmed, and did know beyond any wonderment that they had been chosen to live...and there were not many. They gathered in a place overlooking the sea, and the sea changed before them, and beneath the sea was a land cultivated and teeming with brilliance. They would not have believed, except for their senses, which they trusted because of surviving the holocaust, and they went down to the water, and it parted as they entered and they were not wet.

Into a great kingdom they went, with no fanfare and no disturbance, and they did live in an unnatural place for them that was all the earth was promised and was not. They did begin to find in the deep, the

Heavens, and in the waters, the Earth, and in the waves the music they had needed. And this was so, and cannot be doubted.

The wonder is not that it happened, but that so few went on the journey, for the promise of the soul is not redemption in a distant ungreen land, but the living here, in the Light.

And the Light did follow to the deepness, and there was no shadow. The shadow falls on land from clouds that are warnings of the coming message, and the readiness is in few, and no peace is in the many. And so be it, for to begin again is surely better than erasure of all.

I was stunned. The biblical tone was as foreign to me as Arabic. I felt a sense of shame at having written such a thing, yet, in some unknown place, something in me stirred and moved, like a tiny creature struggling to surface.

For once, I made no attempt to analyze it. I preferred not to interpret this spool of writing which had unrolled so easily under my hand as I'd stared at the paper, the evening news still blaring in the room.

I got up, fixed dinner, said nothing to my family.

The next day I asked: Paul, can you explain the meaning of what was written last night?

It is evident in the words and no need is there for more.

Do you mean that the holocaust has happened? Or is it to come?

It is to come, and much has happened already to show the wise the course. It will not happen in this span, but warnings will disturb the tranquillity for those who heed these things.

What shall we do then?

There is nothing to be done. It is written.

I wrote nothing more that night. The shock of the obviously new voice left me tired and I went to bed early.

In the morning, I knew I needed to find some answers, and made time after car pools and housework to ask:

Who are you? What are you?

I am that which was, and is yet.

I am that which speaks to your highest self, and knows of the shadows.

I am neither in your world, nor yet done with it.

I am a servant of the Source, as you are, but at a different level.

Well, why can I hear you? Why me?

You hear because there is no barrier in you to that which is a higher order.

Any more about you?

I did walk with the Master, and walk there still. The Path was not easy for me, nor for others. It be not necessary for it to be easy—only followed, for it leads to the mountaintop... that which is the connection between one world and the other.

Forms

Ely Leigh arrived early for our lunch date and found me struggling with a heavy steam carpet cleaner that I had rented for the day. As I turned off the machine, I lurched into a sharp corner of the bookcase and yelped in pain. A bruise made its location known immediately, and I knew I'd have a large, discolored lump for weeks.

"Sit down and I'll work on you," Ely said. She placed one of her hands on the bruise, and I gave myself silent permission to let go of the pain and allow myself to heal, unmarked.

Her hand was very hot, yet it seemed to cool me. When she took it away a few minutes later, the bruise had gone down considerably and was barely throbbing.

"Thanks," I said. "That really helped."

"I don't remember much from acupressure class; mostly just do whatever feels right, and trust myself." Our common interests had enhanced our long-standing friendship, and now I regularly did automatic writing for her, and she practiced laying-on of hands on me.

"Are you ready to eat?" I asked. "The salad is all ready—I just need to add the dressing and toss it."

49

"I'll do it," she said, and took the bowl out of the refrigerator and put it on the counter.

I looked down at my dirty hands and two newly broken nails, and looked up to tell her I'd be back in a minute after washing my hands and face. Before I could get the words out of my mouth, she turned toward me and I saw an incredible sight: Ely had a 'picture' coming out of her mouth, encased in an amorphous, pearly grey border that dissolved as I began to yell, "ELY, I SEE IT! I *SEE* WHAT YOU'RE GOING TO SAY!"

Before she could utter a word I said, "You had a picture coming out of you that had a perfect image of the back yard of my old house. You were thinking of that house—but we haven't talked about it in years!"

She stared at me, unable to say anything.

"I didn't *read* your mind—I *saw* what you were thinking! What's that called now? Oh, yes...a thought form!"

"You're absolutely right! I *was* thinking of your old yard, though I don't know why. It certainly doesn't look like this one. Boy, are you getting psychic!" It was scary, but definitely interesting. I wondered what would happen if I saw thought-forms I didn't want to see. Suppose I saw things that people wanted to keep hidden, or things I shouldn't know?

Months later, another bizarre incident occurred. I was sound asleep, having a vivid but unremembered dream, when I awoke with a start to find someone standing at the foot of my bed.

It was just about daybreak, and the room was shades of grey; darkness lingered in the corners and the morning sunlight had not yet begun to filter through the shutters.

The figure was partially turned away from our bed, as though looking toward the closet rather than at Larry and me. I opened my mouth to scream—and no sound came out. I was speechless with fright, sure we were being robbed.

Yet there was something very strange about the shape: I saw the outline of the doorknob through the form, which was neither transparent nor solid, but had an indefinable quality somewhere in between, rather like a figure perceived in a dense fog.

It was dressed in a white T-shirt and jeans; the short hair could have belonged to either a man or a woman, and I still couldn't see the face. Suddenly it turned, and seemed as frightened of me as I of it. It looked like a young man, and a barefoot one at that, for I saw a flash of white feet as it ran from our room.

The normally creaky floors made no sound. Our dog, Moose, didn't bark. Something had happened, but what? I was trembling and perspiring.

In the morning there was no sign of anyone. Larry offered no comment. I was fearful that the thing would return, and this time, instead of running, stay.

Hesitatingly, I told a friend. "Why don't you do your writing and ask who it was?" she suggested.

"I didn't think of that. Good idea."

It took me a day to calm down. When I asked Paul, the answer came back:

> *It was a character in a play unknown to you, not an intruder on a physical plane, but a soul needing your help. Be careful of such beings lest they become attached—their place is not here. He wanders everywhere, but will not harm you if you take him in.*

What shall I say or do to protect myself?

> *Say that you are not available to him at this time and place. Tell him to seek the help of those on his level. This is not you. You are protected—he is not.*

Does he have a name?

> *Not now in your realm... David was his name and he was killed in the jungle war, surprised in the plants— unburied, untended.*

Any more?

> *The fear in you is of the unknown. It is not to be feared.*

That sounded like baloney to me.

I could pretend that the apparition had not happened, and negate an experience I absolutely knew I'd had; I could dismiss it as a dream, yet I knew it was not; I could discount the writing, and end up trusting it less. There was no answer, and I was a woman who liked things neatly tied and labeled.

Several months later, I attended my first holistic conference. One of the speakers was Elisabeth Kübler-Ross, a woman known for her interest in the death experience. She held the audience of 1200 in her small hands as she spoke of her life and her belief in life after death. When she finished, no one was unmoved, least of all me.

I couldn't find words to express all the wonder and awe I felt at her humanitarian approach to death and dying. She had not permitted taping of her hour-long speech and I wanted to hear her, over and over again.

A young woman turned to me and said, ''I'm sure glad I got a tape of her speech last year at Berkeley. It's similar to what she said today.''

''I'd give anything to hear it,'' I said.

''I'll be glad to let you copy it. Come to my room about eight tonight, bring a recorder and a ninety-minute blank cassette. I just don't want to let it out of my hands, but you're certainly welcome to tape in my room.''

''Thanks. That's fantastic!''

Toward the end of the speech I heard Kübler-Ross say, ''Some of you who are sensitives may have an apparition come to you. Many young men who died in Viet Nam are still 'in limbo,' and have not yet found their new plane. Don't be afraid; they're lost. Just send them on their way with love.''

I didn't want to have freakish experiences I could neither control nor understand. At least with the writing, *I* made the choice of bringing through words, even if I didn't know what they'd be. I only wanted to experience what could be understood at some rational level, even if that meant ascribing to Paul an outlet for deeply buried subconscious thoughts.

I needn't have worried. I never saw another thought-form or apparition.

Beliefs

I thought a great deal about what had happened in the five years since I'd so casually taken the first self-hypnosis class.

I couldn't escape looking at my blatant delight in being recognized as 'special.' It was painful to realize how insecure I must be to bask in the attention I got for doing automatic writing, being psychic and healing headaches. I didn't want to quit. I felt like a more interesting person since the phenomena had inexplicably begun, yet discordant notes lurked below the surface excitement—fear of making a fool of myself or, worse still, having the paranormal experiences stop altogether.

Why had it all begun? Was there some unknown task ahead for which I'd have need of Paul's writing to guide me? Where was the dividing line between intuition and other, deeper knowledge? Did everyone have this hidden well of wisdom? The questions were endless, unanswerable. They all led to "why me?" At times I felt as though I were blindfolded and being marched to a new country.

I found it difficult to dwell too long on the vastness of the new land. It was overwhelming in its potential, its unfamiliar

terrain. So many old, firmly entrenched beliefs were eroding so quickly I was not always able or willing to look at the debris of former convictions about God, life, death, life after death. My agnosticism was blasted by the bombshell experiences of ESP, precognition, healing, and—most of all—Paul.

I wanted to isolate the meanings behind the events, but I couldn't seem to separate the experiences from my judgments. My opinions were always there, like huge boulders barring a clear view of the road ahead. Worse, my critical mind was inevitably entwined with emotions, and these emotions were as much a part of me as my fingers; neither opinions nor emotions allowed for a dispassionate perspective.

I could find no logic, no reason, for the paranormal events in my life, but they *had* happened. My old beliefs seemed inadequate for providing exact knowledge about these experiences. But if I listened to the writing, it spoke endlessly from a bedrock of faith I did not feel, did not consciously direct. I could not explain the Christian references when I had been born a Jew, and felt uncomfortable with the increasingly spiritual tone. How could I discuss it with others when what flowed under my hands felt so strange? I was afraid of becoming a 'kook,' fearful of being a fraud. I wrote and wrote, and filed the papers away in an unmarked binder.

Still, in those moments, often months apart, when some deep part of me touched a hidden chord in others, whether through the writing or healing, I was suffused with a new kind of energy I had not felt before. The bond was a link in a chain forged of human connections; and the bond did not bind, but was freeing.

As long as none of it interfered in my relationship with Larry, I encouraged it. I would have given up all the changes if I had been forced to make a choice between marriage and metaphysics.

Of course, that wouldn't happen; Larry said he enjoyed all the new things I was learning—even Paul's writing. Much of his interest came, I was sure, because I had healed his bursitis.

He was my love; nothing else could ever be as important.

Mother

The Bodhi Tree Bookstore in West Hollywood became my favorite haunt; I loved to drink their tea, listen to the wonderful, unfamiliar music playing softly through each room of the old Spanish house, and browse among books on philosophy, psychology, healing, religion. I never came away without buying some.

I had always thought that if I studied more, knew more, I could explain the riddles of life. No matter that the great minds had spent lifetimes doing what I did in my spare time: I wanted to answer my own questions. I simply could not understand how, if there were a God, he permitted events like the Holocaust to happen. Why did He let innocent children die, accidents occur? It was easier to be an agnostic and shrug my shoulders in an "I don't know" than to defend a belief in God and an orderly universe.

The books on Eastern religions intrigued me with their different approach to life. When I'd first studied acupressure and learned of the Oriental concept of the fluidity of life, I didn't see how one could, in actual fact, become accepting and suspend judgment. I'd been taught that it was important to BE judgmental. The exercise of one's critical mind to develop good taste in speech or art or dress was a talent to be encouraged and developed.

Since both my parents were involved with women's fashions, it was a fact of life and breath that I was to be observant in noting color and form, assessing figures and fashions. Criticism and its kinder cousin, evaluation, tended to fill every void. Merely looking at people coming out of the airport while I waited for Larry became, instead of an idle game, a critical one. I never questioned it. Developing "good taste" was an exercise that filled more hours than I would have admitted possible. It was like doing a crossword puzzle to sharpen one's mind.

But the time came when every belief was called up and re-examined, and I could not remain dispassionate.

My mother began to suffer visibly from the effects of arteriosclerosis of the brain. My father and I knew it before she did. The signs were there, written faintly at first: small memory lapses that began to compound until she could no longer remember that she could not remember.

There were periods when she was fine, but she found she could no longer do the books for their business. Worse, she began to lose track of what she actually said or just thought, and would inadvertently insult people who had been long-time customers at their lovely clothing store. She had always been the kindest, most tactful person, and now she alternated between the person she had been and this new entity, unknown and frightening, who might speak her thoughts and say, "Oh, we don't have anything that would look good on a person as overweight as you."

One day while out doing errands in the family car, she became lost, driving farther and farther away, unable to remember the telephone number at the store. At last, the combination clicked in her brain and she called my father to come get her, sure he would be there as he had always been there, although she didn't know where she was and was crying too hard to read the street signs.

The disease encroached insidiously, month by month. Her memory lapses came closer together. She could no longer drive, and now might step into a busy street and say to herself, "They'll stop. They know me." The cars screeching to a halt were not in her world.

Her brain, without its normal oxygen supply, was an unpredictable maze. To outsiders, she appeared a little crazy. To us, she looked so handsome, so elegant, so much younger than her seventy years that it was hard to believe anything could alter her permanently.

My father bore the full brunt of her worsening condition. It was a bravura solo, practiced daily during the long downhill slide of her illness. Helplessly, he watched the death by inches, the grey death, left with the ache and the responsibility.

I lived 400 miles away. I made myself visit, screaming silently, "That's not my mother!" I was terrified that it might happen to me. I said nothing.

Of course they went to doctors. For every malady there was a pill or a treatment, a permanent or temporary remedy—except for this: Alzheimer's disease—utter, devastating senility.

My father hired a succession of 'housekeepers' to be certain his beloved wife would be taken care of while he went to work. My mother sat on the sofa with a stranger she resented, hands clasped in her lap, alternating between staring blankly out the window or crying until she forgot what the tears were for. In moments of lucidity, she knew she was useless. Useless! After a lifetime of loving, of hard work, of surviving, she'd become, inexplicably, unable to function properly. She slept to fill the void where memory used to live.

One night she went into their walk-in closet to find a robe. My father, missing her for an unaccustomed length of time, went looking for her. She was sitting on the floor like a small child, crying.

"What's wrong?" he asked, helping her to her feet.

"I'm lost," she said. "Where am I?"

She, who had always done everything for her husband, could no longer be trusted to even fix a simple breakfast. She put the butter on the flame, forgetting the pan.

He did not know how to fry eggs.

Her huge hazel eyes became like those of a wounded animal. I flew to Las Vegas to see her, to hold her hand and tell her that I loved her. She didn't notice my red, weeping eyes. I didn't cry in her presence, but locked myself in the bathroom if I couldn't stop the tears, sobbing in anger and in sorrow that this was happening to my mother. I had become parent to an aging child, and I hated it. I raged at seeing the life dribble out of her, at the undignified end to a stately life. I remembered her telling me, years earlier, "I've been frightened all of my life—and I still don't know what I've been afraid of." I thought I knew, believed suddenly that in our beginnings we do know our endings: my mother had seen the end, and could not look it in the eye. I was sure the name of the fear was: HELPLESSNESS.

I questioned doctors, healers, psychics. I read books, medical and holistic. All of them, so ready with answers, had no response to this creeping senility that wove its paralyzing web around her.

Now it worsened...by the day, by the hour.

She became suddenly, silently frail, in danger of falling down the stairs, of burning herself. She didn't always remember how to dress or bathe; on her worst days, she couldn't even recall how to go to the bathroom, much less find it. She rarely spoke, because she couldn't remember what words meant, could not string them together. She listened to the record player, head nodding slowly, as though she remembered the classics she had played before audiences a half century before.

My father and I, each in our own way, raged at an unfair fate: he, in sudden bursts of anger; I, in lonely writing during sleepless hours. I marveled that he didn't break under the strain. His loving wife was now a grey wraith with blank eyes and clutching hands.

So many, many years of being a loving wife and mother, and we had to put her in a 'convalescent' hospital, to end as a shriveled, mindless shell of a human being, tied to a chair, never to walk in the sun or recall the names of her loved ones.

Why? *Why?* WHY?

One day I visited her hospital room, held her hands and looked into her beautiful, empty eyes. A kind of understanding passed through me, softening the pain just a little. She, who had been so fastidious, so immaculate, was sitting in her own filth and didn't know it. Her body was dead to her. She, who had worried and taken into her being every kind and unkind word ever spoken to her, could remember nothing. The few words she could manage usually came out in an undecipherable stutter, endlessly repetitive. Yet this day she smiled and clutched at my hands, and managed to say the words, "I love you."

In my desperate search for a cure, for help, I saw the futility of it all: here sat my mother, with the trappings of culture, discipline, manners, wisdom... gone. And I knew all that was left was her soul—her spirit—shining still in her eyes and radiating from her ungovernable hands. Everything else was lost, would be lost forever.

I fancied that I saw the swing of the pendulum of life: that unfathomable metronome of existence that defied explanation and was, perhaps, more frightening than the unknown. I thought of death not as a black void, but a respite from the pains of life, or at least the pain of its ending. I could not judge her dying any more than I could judge my living; I could only see the light in her eyes, feel the blood pulsing in her hands, and know she still responded to a hug and a kiss and a smile. If I did not shake my fist at an uncaring God, if I did not judge her as she was, there was so much, still, to love.

Moss

I was commissioned to do a magazine article about Dr. Thelma Moss, including interview and pictures. She was a pioneer in the investigation and reporting of the entire field of parapsychology. Her book, *The Probability of the Impossible*, was a basic text covering the historical background and current work in the diverse aspects of the paranormal, including ESP, precognition, and Kirlian photography.

Most of the medical colleagues at UCLA were hostile toward her and her work; anything that deviated from the established medical model was suspect, and anything that happened outside the scientific method was thought to be fraudulent, despite paranormal experiences reported in every culture, through every era.

But the university did provide Dr. Moss a forum to conduct a semester-long class, named after her book. I enrolled along with several friends, and Larry promised to attend when he could.

Several hundred people filled the lecture hall for the first class meeting. Dr. Moss introduced Kendall Johnson, an associate who had helped set up the controversial Kirlian laboratory, a process claiming to show the 'auras' of things.

"Ken is going to conduct an informal experiment," she began in her deep, throaty voice. "Everyone who wishes may participate. I don't know the subject whose work you'll be asked to describe, so I'm just an interested observer for this part of our class."

Ken stepped to the microphone and gave us our instructions. "I've selected an artist, who, on each of three successive Sundays—between noon and 3 p.m.—will work on a piece of art. You're to 'tune in' psychically to this artist to see if you can determine where the artist is working, what medium is used, and the subject and composition of the picture. If possible, draw a sketch of your impressions. Write down any and all details, no matter how odd they seem. Put your name on the paper and we'll collect them as you come into class Tuesday night. After you've turned them in, I'll show the artwork to you; however, the artist won't appear in person until the fourth Tuesday, when he or she will answer all your questions. Obviously, this is a very casual experiment. Use anything you can think of that works to help you with extra-sensory perception."

On Sunday I was so busy painting my bathroom that I forgot the whole thing. Ely Leigh, who was in Dr. Moss' class too, called and urged me to hypnotize myself to see what information I could get.

I lay down, but my restless mind couldn't get a "fix" on the artist's location. I couldn't visualize beach, mountains, desert or studio. All I sensed was a triangular composition with cliffs in the background and a feeling that the picture represented the artist looking out from this environment to the viewer. I had no idea what medium was used.

It appeared as though many in the class turned in papers two days later. Ken showed us an oil painting in which a face was looking at the viewer. There were vague cliffs painted in the background. He assured us it was not a self-portrait of the artist, although I was sitting so far back in the auditorium I couldn't have described the face. I had written other details which were inaccurate, and overall I felt I'd done poorly; perhaps next week would be better.

The following Sunday I was deeply involved in an extremely difficult photographic assignment. Ely called once again to remind me of our experiment, and I gladly agreed to take a break to do it. Again, I was unable to relax, got little additional information and felt I wasn't able to use whatever powers I had. I sensed that the picture this week represented a cave-like place; the composition was still triangular, the subject undefined except that it was looking at me.

Tuesday night, Ken produced a picture of a cave that the artist had photographed in Machu Picchu, Peru. The composition was somewhat triangular. Ken asked for a show of hands from those who had any 'direct hits.'

There were a few. When he called on me, I said, "I got the cave, but while I did feel the composition was triangular, it's similar to last week's picture, although done in a different medium."

Thelma Moss was seated in the front row while Ken was on stage and she said, "Bobbie, that was a bit of precognition in tuning in to the image of the cave."

I blurted out, "Well, there's a little more. It sounds silly, but it's been on my mind all week, and I can't figure out how it relates to my life other than—perhaps—this experiment." I could feel my face redden with every eye on me as I stood addressing Ken and Dr. Moss at the front of the hall. "I can't seem to get *apples* out of my mind. I don't particularly like to eat them, and I certainly don't ever think about apples, other than this week, when they kept popping up like a refrain from a tune I couldn't stop humming. Could this be connected to the artist in some way?"

Ken shook his head. "I don't know. You'll have to wait two more weeks to ask that question directly."

On the third Sunday, I was ready and very willing to do the experiment and be open to whatever came through, but there was nothing—nothing at all except an image of a hat or helmet with ear-flaps. When Ken showed the new piece of art the following Tuesday, it seemed I was totally inaccurate. Of course I knew that ESP was unpredictable, but I was disappointed that I hadn't improved. The image of the ear-flapped head covering stayed with me all week although I kept trying to chase it out of my mind.

We were all anticipating the meeting with the unknown artist when the fourth Tuesday class began, but first Dr. Moss passed around a multiple-choice questionnaire about our mystery guest. After we'd turned in our papers and were told the correct answers, I wasn't surprised to find that I had not done particularly well—answering about half of the questions correctly. They were, after all, multiple choice, so I assumed that the law of averages must help the respondent.

At last the artist appeared to answer questions from the audience. I gathered up my courage to stand and ask, "Do apples have anything to do with the Machu Picchu photograph?"

He stared at me for an uncomfortable length of time and I wanted desperately to sit down and—better yet—disappear. Suddenly he said, "Oh, my God!" then paused again before he was able to continue. "I had dreamt all my life of going into the jungle to visit the one spot on earth I wanted to see more than any other...the ancient Inca ruins of Peru. When I finally got the money together and made my reservations for the trip, I was told there was only one isolated hotel from which I could explore the area that fascinated me so. I had no sooner registered at the hotel after the long journey when every employee went out on strike. There was nowhere else for me to go. Hotel guests had no service of any kind. That didn't really bother me, but we had no food because the restaurant help walked out too." Prickles began to float up my spine. "There was nothing at all to eat. Except apples. I lived on apples for three days. No one has ever known that, and I'd forgotten all about it until you mentioned 'apples' in connection with the photo of me in the cave."

Dr. Moss jumped to her feet and shouted, "Bobbie, that's incredible!" The audience was murmuring and I felt hot-faced and very proud. I debated briefly about retiring in momentary glory or risking it with another question. I stayed on my feet and heard myself say, "One more thing. I've had the strangest image all week of a hat or helmet with ear-flaps, and I can't seem to get rid of the picture. Does it fit anywhere for you? It obviously wasn't in any of your artwork."

He said, "That's amazing! Absolutely astounding! I had a photographic assignment I shot yesterday and the main prop was a German World War I helmet with ear-flaps. You must have had the idea before I did!"

Now the large lecture hall was really buzzing and I sat

down, dazed and flattered by my unexpected success. Dr. Moss called for a short break, and people crowded around to congratulate me and ask how I'd done it. I didn't know. The information was just there. I didn't have the power to make it come, nor to make it disappear. If the artist hadn't cleared up the mysteries, I'd have been stuck with apple and ear-flap images forever! While I loved the attention, a little voice inside said that it was utterly unimportant and to let go of the accolades.

I moved away to get a cup of coffee and was confronted by a woman with a tape recorder and microphone.

"You vere vonderful," she said in a heavy German accent. "Vould you conzent to be interviewed by me for ze Bavarian Broadcasting Zystem? My name is Nortrud."

I was sure it was some sort of joke. She asked for my name and phone number and said I'd be hearing from her soon.

A week later, Nortrud called to set a time for the appointment. As soon as she hung up I regretted not taking her phone number, in case I wanted to cancel. I'd never done any paranormal work on demand before, and she had requested that I do some psychic work for her in addition to the interview, which she would tape.

On Friday, she arrived at my home with two men and another woman, who spoke halting English. She had not asked to bring others, and I was annoyed at the distraction they provided.

Nortrud set up her tape recorder and produced a notepad. The other three looked as though they'd just come off a mountain—athletic types, dressed in Tyrolean hiking clothes: heavy boots, shorts, suspenders over bright shirts, and feathered caps. They seemed more curious about my home than the interview, and I felt uncomfortable as their eyes roamed over every item. They were polite, however, and once Nortrud introduced them I felt a bit better.

She asked how I generally got psychic information, and I relayed a bit of my history with automatic writing (although I'd not thought to use it for the class experiment); still, I was sure it had provided an opening of some kind.

"Vill you write for us?"

"Yes. I'll get my pad of paper."

I returned in a moment to find them speaking rapidly in German. They stopped abruptly as I sat on the floor. I liked to write in a relaxed position leaning on an elbow, but now as I looked up, the others towered over me and stared down impassively as I explained slowly, "When I write for others, I never know which person I'll 'pick up.' I'll just begin writing, and after a bit, I'll ask if the information coming through fits anyone."

Well, this will certainly be a test, I thought. Even with Denise studying in her room and our dog locked up with her, I felt like a stranger in my own den. As always, I was fearful that the psychic ability would desert me, leaving me stranded on the shore of my own pretensions.

I closed my eyes, took a deep breath, and my hand began to write. A burial at a small cemetery, a long walk home, and

A FIRE! A FIRE!

printed in large letters. The image of a stone tower, rather like a land-bound lighthouse, appeared—it was quite unlike anything I'd ever seen. It felt like a place of refuge for a lonely child, and I saw a young person playing a reed instrument high up in the round building. Suddenly, the scene dissolved and I picked up the image of a teacher rapping knuckles hard and saying in a mean voice, "Don't you forget. Don't you ever forget!" Speaking quietly as I told them what my hand was writing, I described a girl, a dog, and suddenly the one they called Lorenz began crying softly and saying, "It is me, it is all me, and I was that lonely boy and the teacher did do that and it was all correct, most correct. It happened in Germany when I was about seven."

The phone rang and I jumped up to answer it. Larry was calling from Omaha, Nebraska.

"Hi, honey," he said. "How are you? What's new?"

"Right now I'm being interviewed by the Bavarian Broadcasting System," I said, having difficulty not lapsing into an accent.

"Sure you are. What are you doing—really? You sound kind of funny. How's Denny? Have you heard from Linda?" We talked a bit, then I went back to the den and sat down with my pen and paper.

"Don't you have to go into a trance?" Nortrud asked.

"No. I just have to quiet down on the inside." I wrote again, and this time the words told me of a different life:

> She walked up and it was very cold that winter and the floor heater didn't work good and she did say I will get out and she did. And she left the Christmas party.

Nortrud said, "That is me. That is accurate."

I wrote a bit more and then the writing stopped. The four spoke among themselves before Nortrud began speaking into the tape recorder. She told me she was recapping what I'd written and said for them.

They all stood up at once, said a polite goodbye, and left.

I was enthralled with these events that were happening to me, but apprehensive too. I could, it seemed, discover trivia that had happened in the past to strangers in a country I'd never visited—extrasensory perception. I'd been able to 'see' what an artist would use as a subject before he himself had selected it. If I developed and practiced this power—precognition—would I be able to do it more often? Even when I wasn't concentrating? Could I *really* 'see' into the future? And, most crucial of all, did I *want* to do more, know more? Was I overstepping some ill-defined boundary into the unknown that would bring more pain than joy?

The most terrifying movie I'd ever seen (which had given me nightmares for weeks), had been about psychic powers. A man, gaining possession of a magic ring, had suddenly seen a cross on the forehead of those who would die soon, and the knowledge eventually drove him mad and caused his death.

When I was innocent of such knowledge really existing in this world, I dismissed the movie as scary fiction. But now, new worlds of possibilities were opening up that could reveal the past and, occasionally, the future. I knew I wanted to continue to work in it, even at my amateurish level, but I was afraid I might have the ability to predict life and death, and I did not want to possess such knowledge.

Ghosts

Excitement, mystery, and the unpredictability of PSI events, coupled with my now inflated ego, combined to lure me deeper into this intriguing new world. I still maintained my normal life of family, friends, and mini-career in photography. I managed a traditional housewife-in-the-suburbs role although nearly everyone who knew of my growing interest in the paranormal thought it was 'weird.' My studies and automatic writing helped balance the loneliness of Larry's increasing preoccupation with business and his need to travel more and more.

Thelma Moss had mentioned the name of Barry Taff with respect, which was more than the *Los Angeles Times* had done. They wrote him up and put him down as a frustrated ghost hunter and haunted house inspector. I heard that he conducted free sessions at UCLA exploring ESP, so Ely Leigh and I decided to go. The announcement instructed us to meet in the main waiting room of the enormous UCLA Neuropsychiatric Institute (NPI). I was glad Ely was with me, for from the very beginning, the evening felt odd.

More than a dozen people had assembled and now stared at Barry as he introduced himself and asked us to follow him to a meeting room. No one spoke as our footsteps echoed down the seemingly endless labyrinth of corridors. Ely and I walked next to Barry, towering over him. I had the feeling that either he'd been thrown in the washing machine and shrunk, or we'd been stretched to gigantic proportions. My 5'6" height seemed, momentarily, huge.

At last we came to a small, glaringly lit room with a tight circle of colorful chairs surrounding a microphone on a stand. Barry said, "Well, it's happened again. I set up sixteen chairs this afternoon, and that's exactly how many of us showed up."

He sat down next to me and described the procedure. "After we take a few minutes to relax and center ourselves, I'll select someone to be a 'sender.' The rest of you will be 'receivers.' The sender will pick a subject who is very well known to him personally—not a prominent public figure. The subject must be human—no pets allowed here—alive, and adult. The sender will mention only the first name of the subject, and then concentrate on that person in silence. As we get information, we, the receivers, will spontaneously give our impressions, so speak up, yell, shout it out! The microphone and tape recorder will pick up everything we say. When I call time, our sender will rewind the tape and play back our words, stopping the tape and commenting on our hits or misses."

Barry turned off the lights. We all joined hands and did our deep breathing and relaxation in the dark. It all seemed so funny—I felt like a little kid at a Halloween party waiting for something scary to bump into me. It seemed "stagey" and the dark silence began to stretch interminably. Finally, Barry disengaged his hand from mine and moved to turn the lights up slightly. He handed the tape recorder to a man he had evidently selected as the sender.

The man said, "Robert."

Suddenly, I began to squirm. It felt as though the walls were closing in. I was disoriented, lonely, frightened...and caged. I spoke up in a voice that sounded strange to me: "I'm in a cell. There's a bare light bulb hanging over my cot. I think I'm going crazy! Even my plaid shirt is driving me crazy!" I was surprised at the sound of my strong, panicky voice. I glanced at my sweater, relieved to find I wasn't wearing a plaid shirt. I was not in a trance, and was very much aware of the other people in the room, but no one indicated that what I had said was peculiar. The sender listened impassively as others spoke up. Voices cropped out from all around the circle, interrupting each other at times; occasionally there were long silences. Some people gave specific information—places, dates, events in the subject's life. Barry, especially, spoke in a strong, positive voice. Some spoke tentatively, weakly, halting and searching for words. I had nothing more to add, and I felt oppressed, imprisoned.

Finally, Barry called "time." He turned the fluorescent lights up to an uncomfortable level and the sender rewound the tape. As he played it back, I heard my own voice describing the fear I'd felt.

When my portion of the tape ended, he said, "Robert is my uncle. He was in solitary confinement in a cell in a mental institution, knowing he was going crazy, contemplating suicide. The cell had one bare light bulb. The description of him wearing a plaid shirt is absolutely correct."

A small part of me wanted approval and acknowledgment but the greater part wasn't at all relieved that I had tuned in so well; I felt depressed and nothing seemed light or pleasurable at that moment.

We heard the whole tape and Barry said, "I estimate that we were about 60% correct. That's just fair. We can do much better."

Again he lowered the lights, we relaxed, and another person 'sent' a new subject, who came through jumbled and less defined than the first one. I still felt oppressed and said nothing, aware only of confusion. Suddenly, my right hand, with Barry's small hand in mine, began jumping uncontrollably. I had an overpowering, embarrassing urge to hit someone. I muttered, "I want to hit him! I'm going to hit him!" I was angry now, jabbing at an unseen assailant. "No one appreciates my artistic talents here. I'm going to hit you, hit you, hit you!"

The surge of anger disappeared as suddenly and mysteriously as it had come. Barry got up to adjust the lights, and I was left staring at my sweating palms tightly clutched in my lap.

The subject, a cousin of the sender, was an artist who had been drafted into the army and sent to Viet Nam. He'd been there quite a while, apparently disintegrating mentally, when he erupted—accosting and socking a prominent South Vietnamese official. Our subject had been court-martialed and dishonorably discharged.

We took a much needed break for coffee. When we regrouped, I felt that the essences of the disturbed people who'd been 'sent' were still present, so I asked Barry if I could 'send' someone: my friend Elynor Hart—a happy, harmonious person. I thought her image might counteract the depressed atmosphere that pervaded the room.

Barry called on someone else, and for the third time I was plunged into the depths.

A strange feeling crept through me. I began to feel my body infiltrated by a grunching, grinding force, nebulous at first, rather like a heavy, dense fog that became darker and deeper, dangerously crowding out my breath, although just a moment ago I'd been fine. The heaviness condensed in my chest and I burst out, "I can't breathe, I can't breathe! Help me, help me!" My mouth was open, gasping for air, my nostrils open as wide as I could get them. Frantically, I wanted to get out of the room, but I did not have the power to even get out of my chair. I was ready to scream when the compression eased off and I was able to take shallow, quick breaths that relieved the panic. Others were speaking as though nothing had happened, giving information about the subject's life in factual terms.

When the lights came on and the tape replayed, the sender told us that she had 'sent' her father, a writer who was going through a deep depression and was unable to work. He complained constantly of massive chest pains and was sure he was having heart attacks. He didn't believe the doctors who had checked him thoroughly and told him that all his physical symptoms, including his shortness of breath and severe chest pains, were imaginary. His test results were those of a healthy man, so they said.

I was thankful to be with a friend who had but a few sharp glimpses into the depressing lives that had been sent. She was relatively untouched by the evening; I was devastated by the experience.

From what I'd heard during our brief coffee break, all of us were amateurs at exploring ESP except Barry, yet I was the only one who seemed to pick up emotional states rather than more factual data. My body reverberated with the pain of these three lives and I prayed that a good night's sleep would wipe away memory of the evening as an eraser deletes class-work from a blackboard.

But I did not sleep well. Shifting, tumbling thoughts framed questions I could not answer: what good was sensitivity or psychic ability if it would affect my life in a negative way? Why had this door been opened? The trivia I'd picked up before seemed preferable to the feelings of disoriented person-alities projected in Barry's experiment. In the future, I would choose what situations I got into more carefully.

What had changed? Or had I?

Strings

I became friendly with a cousin I'd never known before she moved to Los Angeles. Lorraine shared some of my interests; she attended Dr. Moss' class with me and enjoyed it immensely. One night, she brought an out-of-town friend to the lecture and asked if I'd do some writing for them later on.

I agreed, and after class Lorraine and her friend, Helen, came to my house.

I told them I didn't want to know anything about Helen before I began to write, so we playfully kept her from talking and revealing any personal facts. We settled down in the living room with some wine, in a silly, light-hearted mood even before drinking.

I sat on the sofa facing them, a pad of newsprint on my lap, waiting for words.

At first I wrote of generalities that could have fit anyone. Then the writing shifted to a well-defined scene of a schoolyard. There was a young girl, taunted by her schoolmates, being pushed out of a swing and cutting her knees badly on the ground.

"That happened to me," Helen said.

I wrote

aspen trees

and described a home surrounded by them.

"Me, again," Helen said.

Suddenly I felt cold. Pain seeped into my chest and I had difficulty breathing. I shut my eyes to help focus the increasing discomfort.

"What's wrong?" Lorraine asked.

"I'm getting a sense that one of you has had your life threatened by some respiratory problem. Has either of you had pneumonia? Anything related to breathing problems?"

They shook their heads. "No."

I wanted to write but words wouldn't come. Only feelings, feelings of panic as though I couldn't get enough air. My hands were pressed tightly to my chest; I was breathing hard, gasping for air, in some bizarre drama not of my life—I was acting out a part without knowing the plot.

"Are you OK?" Lorraine asked in a concerned voice.

"No. Yes. I don't know..."

I prayed it wouldn't be a repeat of the NPI experiment, but it felt as though I was picking up illness again. I was frightened.

"Are you sure neither of you ever had any symptoms like this?"

Again, no.

I wrote a few words until an even stronger sensation made my hands leap involuntarily to my neck. I tried to protect myself from the overwhelming feeling that I was being choked. I gasped for breath, rocking back and forth, aware I was playing out some horrible death manifesting itself through me. But whose? Why?

Lorraine said, "Bobbie, please stop. I've never seen you like this, and really—it isn't important that you write for us if you're going to go through such misery."

I shut my eyes again so I wouldn't be distracted by them, by the room. I needed to get in touch with something new that was happening, get control of myself. "I have to go on.

I must find out how this relates to either one of you. I'm afraid that if I don't, I'll be stuck with this terrible energy. I don't understand it, but I can't believe it's inaccurate when the feelings are so powerful.''

I sensed I was more keenly attuned to Helen while she continued to deny a good part of what my hand wrote. I became very cold, usually a sure sign I was right 'on.'

I sat silently shivering, staring at the pad of paper. It was as though the windows had been opened and a cold wind was blowing through the living room. I looked up to see if the plant leaves were moving, but all was as it had been, except that Helen and Lorraine were putting on their sweaters.

"It feels like somebody opened a door and is in here with us," Lorraine said in a small voice. "I could swear someone's in this room."

My hand began scribbling in tiny, condensed handwriting—so minute I could hardly read it:

she was beaten

I was embarrassed, not sure whether or not to go on. I wanted to extricate myself from the discomfort, especially the bone-chilling cold, but a strong sense within me said the mystery should be cleared, not ignored.

I asked, "Have either of you ever been beaten?"

Neither spoke. I repeated my question, and added, "I really hate to ask this, but that's what is written."

Lorraine gasped, "Helen! It's your father! Tell her what happened to him!"

Helen began sobbing uncontrollably and couldn't speak. I was upset for her; the happy woman I'd met just a few hours before when we'd blithely decided to have fun with my automatic writing had dissolved into tears.

"Come sit in front of me," I suggested. "I'll do some acupressure that will relax you."

Like a terrified child, she moved closer, waiting to be soothed.

Touching her seemed to help both of us. Within a few minutes, the room warmed, my chest and throat pains stopped, and she was able to tell me what had happened.

"I guess I always loved *and* hated my father," she began. "Like any kid, I really needed his approval. I rarely got it. When I came home from school I never knew whether or not he might hit me. As I got older he started to harrass and abuse me sexually. I seemed to provoke him, no matter what I did. When I was a teenager, I ran away from home to escape him, his beatings and mistreatment. I lived in another state for several years. One day, I received a phone call from my mother, telling me my father had died. She said he'd gotten up in the middle of the night to go to the bathroom, got tangled in the shower curtain cord in the dark, and accidentally strangled to death. At one point, it was suspected he'd also had a heart attack. The police claimed it was suicide. They don't know which it was; because of insurance problems, it even ended in the courts. I only know he was found dead on the floor, the cord wound around his neck. I've spent half my life trying to change my feelings about him. I guess all I did was block out the painful memories. You really acted out his death, and it didn't dawn on me until you mentioned getting beaten."

Lorraine asked an interesting question. "Bobbie, is there anything she can do to clear this up once and for all? Can you ask Paul to answer that?"

My hand wrote:

> When this woman be in another time and place and feeling quiet in her insides, she to be ACTING OUT his life and death with her. By talking to him as though he be alive and there with her, and talking about the cords between them, she must relive some painful times in order to be clearing them. She needs to ask her own questions about their times together in order to free the self from the bonds. She must relive it, and then let go of those strings, that energy.

They left soon afterwards. My psychic abilities had given me no inkling that the evening would be invaded by something dark and painful. I was drained—powerless to control what I'd received and needing protection from emotional connections to others that brought me down.

Dream

A few months after the episodes of involvement with the emotional distress of others, I dismissed those experiences as a passing, inexplicable phase. I no longer manifested physical symptoms when doing automatic writing for others, and I did not return to Barry Taff's weekly gathering.

My life was going smoothly. Linda was away at college, Denny was happy at high school, photography was an ongoing pleasure for me, and I could hardly wait for Larry to come home at night to talk about our experiences.

I also continued a leisurely, random study of PSI phenomena and sporadic laying-on of hands to relieve headaches and minor physical problems.

I had read that dreams provide a rich storehouse of self-knowledge, but my memory of them was erratic. I kept a flashlight and notebook by the bedside so I could record them immediately. It was unusual for me to write very much, although each morning when I awoke, I knew that I had dreamt. Occasionally, I'd have good recall of a dream for two or three consecutive nights, and the only evaluation I could make was that dream memory was enhanced when I was exceptionally open. Falling asleep, I often suggested a dream theme to myself. Once in a while the dream did fulfill the basic request. It was fun to see what would happen without demanding that I remember anything; the easier I was on myself, the more responsive was the dreamer in me.

Several months after Dr. Moss' class ended, I had a dream unlike anything I'd ever experienced before... one which I was unable to forget, much as I wanted to.

Larry and I, exceptionally tired after a particularly busy day, went to bed early one night. As I was slipping into sleep, I asked my subconscious mind to give me a dream that would tell me what I most needed to know.

In the night's dream I had gone to sleep, but was awakened by an urgent sense that I had to get out of bed to make sure that Denny was all right. I turned on lights and hurried down the hall toward her room. Suddenly, all the lights went out. I was stopped by an invisible, horrifying presence. It hovered like a dark, winged thing above the roof and wrapped itself about the house, ready to crush us. I was frozen with fear, unable to take a step or even cry out to Larry. Thoughts of death floated in. What have I done? Why must I die? What crime have I committed to cause this force to surround us like an evil cloud? Although I *knew* the insidious force had come because of me, I was afraid it would consume Denny and Larry and Moose. I had no weapons with which to fight. I saw myself shiver in terror, making pathetic attempts to condense and protect myself, hearing my own panting breaths in my ear. Infinity—an eternity of fear—until the floor released my feet and I was able to move. I felt drawn to the back yard. I passed through the house in a cold silence, opened the back door and stood staring at the eerie shadows of the densely planted shrubbery. Sharp moonlight glittered on the pool, reflected from the metal ribs of outdoor furniture. Nothing moved—neither could I. Once again the sense of impending, close death held me immobilized. I was aware of dark, unfamiliar forms on the far side of the pool: a dog, stiffened by death, lying belly up, eyes bulged in terror with tongue lolling on the ground, and on its lower belly, a dead cat apparently struck down by the same force... the invisible, suffocating death that was about to consume me. It was not my dog, or my neighbor's cat. Was I being given a few last moments to examine my life, perhaps make a plea for mercy? Time passed while I searched for something to do, to say, to delay death. My fear-rooted feet relaxed and I walked back into the silent house. Should I wake Larry and Denny, or let them sleep, perhaps die? If the presence were only after me, if I did not scream and waken them, they might be spared. I didn't know what to do. All that came to my lips was a silly jingle learned in acupressure class and dismissed as rubbish:

> *I am in the Light*
> *I am of the Light*
> *I am protected by the Light.*
> *My aura is sealed.*
> *Nothing can harm me. Nothing can.*

Instantly, every light in the house went on, the presence evaporated, and I woke up sobbing and shaking, with my heart pumping frantically.

Denny was standing in the doorway. "Mom, mom, wake up! What happened? Did you have a nightmare?"

"Oh, my God, did I!" The dream had been so powerful I had trouble realizing I was safe in my own bed with Larry snoring evenly beside me. "Did you just get in? What happened to the lights?"

"What lights? Jeff and I just got home and turned on one light in the den while we talked. Then I heard these weird sounds from your bedroom. That must have been some nightmare."

"It was. Maybe I'll be able to talk about it in the morning."

I didn't write down the dream. I only wanted to erase it, but it was indelibly etched in my mind. The message couldn't have been clearer: I urgently needed to protect myself in the psychic and healing work I was doing. Apparently, it didn't matter that I was a beginner, a non-professional. I was probing the unknown, and didn't know enough to take proper precautions to care for myself. I had dismissed the experiences with Barry Taff and Helen too lightly. Now I would listen!

The next morning, I told Larry and Denny about the dream and my interpretation of it. There was little they could say, for the terror had been all mine—Larry hadn't even awakened. They didn't doubt that it had been a realistic nightmare, but it had nothing to do with their lives.

After breakfast, I went out in the hot, sunny back yard to do some cleanup and watering and noticed some flowers dying in a planter. They were getting too much sun; it had to be moved. I asked Denny to help me, and together we struggled to carry the unwieldy tub to the shadier side of the yard. As we passed by the back door I noticed something half-hidden by a chair. It couldn't be what I thought! When we put down the planter, I said, "Thanks, honey. Come over here for just a minute, will you?" I wanted a witness.

Lying by the chair was a small dead bird. It lay rigid, belly-up to the sky, beak and eyes open, tiny legs stiff. There were no dog or cat teethmarks on it.

"Mom—my God, it's just like your dream!"

One world had intruded upon another. Once more, the message was being punched home. Another warning—this one tangible, provable, real...and very, very dead.

I hadn't paid attention to books that mentioned the dark side of intuitive and psychic gifts, but one or two intense experiences meant more than a whole library of reading material. I knew now—without doubt—that my unconscious had its dark side, which attuned to that part in others. If I denied that this was so, I would never be able to understand human nature; I had best learn to trust myself to maintain a calm inner center, no matter what might happen.

It was, as always, easier said than done.

Talisman

In April, 1977, I attended a conference about healing that offered an opportunity to take an eight-hour workshop with Oh Shinnah Fastwolf, a beautiful woman of Apache-Scottish heritage. She reflected a serenity I found very appealing.

Oh Shinnah wore an Indian dress and braided her long hair with beads. Her Scottish ancestry had diluted her skin, eye, and hair colors to medium shades of brown.

I was one of fifteen who formed a semicircle around her. She spoke with reverence of the Indian's relationship to nature and her tribe's trust in medicine men or women as healers. It was a paradoxical evening; we listened to her vibrant contralto voice speak and sing of the earth while we sat in a huge, red-carpeted, richly paneled room in the Biltmore Hotel in downtown Los Angeles.

From comments I overheard after class, not everyone found her as enchanting as I did. A few said her Indian philosophy was alien and her stories irrelevant to their lives. I had always been fascinated with Indian lore, and was excited about the second session which would, she said, include an Apache healing ritual.

The following night, the meeting was held in a small, drab room, more appropriate in size for our group. The conference leaders decided to tape our session, much to Oh Shinnah's disgust, for she considered the harsh lighting and video cameras an intrusion.

I volunteered to carry some equipment from another room.

"Look, lady, this is expensive stuff. Are you sure you're strong enough?" David, the video man, spoke curtly. I took his comments as a personal affront even though he was rude to everyone, arrogantly ordering us all to move.

When we finally were settled down, Oh Shinnah reviewed some Indian medicine. She mentioned the belief that certain colors possess healing power for specific diseases. She taught us a simple chant, and said we would practice a healing ritual upon a volunteer. Someone lay down on the floor. I was overwhelmed with an intense, non-specific feeling that something was about to happen which would be very unhealthy for me. Much as I wanted to see what she would do, I excused myself from the room.

Never before had I honored internal warnings so instantly. Two other women who had also left joined me in the hallway.

One woman, outlandish in appearance, identified herself as a professional psychic. She said she, too, had feelings of danger about some force in the room. The other woman had no particular comments and appeared to have followed her friend as a puppy would trail its mother. What an odd situation this is, I thought: we three, waiting like expelled students in a dim hallway in the Biltmore while sounds of Indian chants filtered under the door.

About fifteen minutes later, we were called back to the room. I wanted very much to be a part of the group and listen to Oh Shinnah, but I was prepared to leave again if my sense of danger still persisted.

As I walked back in, I was aware of something having shifted; I wasn't alarmed, but immediately began to feel strong stomach pains that I knew belonged to someone else.

I asked the man on the floor, "Did you—do you—have stomach problems?"

"No," he said.

"I'm really feeling that someone here has severe cramps. Does that fit anyone?" Everyone was looking at me, and none too warmly, I thought.

Oh Shinnah waited patiently, glancing from face to face.

The silence lengthened. At last David spoke in a subdued voice. "I have an ulcer. It wasn't bothering me earlier today, but right now it's killing me. How did you know?"

The feeling in the room altered and I felt a rush of compassion toward David. The moment sympathetic feelings replaced hostility, *my* stomach pains disappeared and I surprised myself by giving him a warm, heartfelt hug.

Oh Shinnah watched the scene, and as David turned back to his camera, she announced we would do one more healing ritual and asked me to lie on the floor. The others clustered about, following her chant as best they could. She asked that a healing green light illuminate my heart. I didn't feel anything special, but it was relaxing to lie down, surrounded by others.

When the group had finished sending energy to me, we resumed our semicircle around Oh Shinnah. I felt centered and receptive, refreshed rather than healed.

Near the end of our session, she paused dramatically and held up a small rock. It was dark in color, small enough to fit in a closed palm, and shaped like a Maltese cross, ends flared.

"I hold something of great importance to my tribe. My greatgrandmother and grandmother, both medicine women, had this rock, as did Cochise, our last great warrior. It was hidden near his grave, waiting, so it was said, for a safer time to be uncovered. My grandmother passed it on to me when she felt the time was ready and I was capable of understanding its strength. It is the medicine rock of my people. I carry it always, and will pass it on in turn to one who knows the way of the Apache, the way of Indian healing. This kind of stone is found in only one place in all the world, and it is a sacred place for my people. I will let you pass it around, but I ask that you hold your palm flat to receive it carefully and allow your neighbor to place the sacred rock gently on your hand. Please observe silence until it passes around the circle and comes back to me."

I noticed different responses as the stone changed hands. Several got rid of it quickly as though it were on fire. A few seemed puzzled, and turned it over to examine it. One or two held it longer than the others, a look of quiet contentment on their faces.

It was handed to me. It was surprisingly heavy for such a small object. I held it in my left hand and placed my right hand over it, and put both hands, rock securely between, to my forehead, fingers pointing up.

I felt a tremendous jolt of energy as though an enormous, split-second earthquake had rocked me. I was instantaneously transported to another time, an unknown place. I felt as though I'd been bodily moved by a vast, benevolent force and taken to a mountaintop, where I sat, stone in hand, surveying the universe. The stone emitted a sense of power and wisdom that was utterly hypnotic; I was uplifted by the ageless peace that radiated from it. I felt possessed of an exquisite under-standing of creation, of unity from this high place that held the knowledge of the mysteries of creation and bestowed full acceptance of everything in it. I was complete, infinite, immortal.

I was aware of the presence of water I couldn't see; some small, rational part of my mind reviewed water as: well, stream, river, lake, ocean, but nothing seemed to fit. This water had no boundaries.

I knew my physical body was in a room in a city, rocking slowly back and forth, holding a stone—but the body was a small, insignificant part of me. The *real me* was sitting on a mountaintop viewing eternity, sustained by unseen water, immeasurably enriched by the stone.

I had no idea how long I held the rock when my focus changed slowly, unwillingly, back to the room. Very reluctantly I gave the rock to my neighbor, the last to receive it.

Oh Shinnah asked for responses to her treasure.

"It felt hot, horrible!" one woman said vehemently. "I couldn't get rid of it quickly enough!"

Another said, "I heard voices coming from it but couldn't understand what they were saying."

A third said, "It was warm. Kind of comforting."

Most spoke. I felt unusually quiet and didn't volunteer a

comment. Oh Shinnah turned to me and said, "I'm sure you must have something interesting to report." I repeated everything I'd sensed, but felt I sounded woefully inadequate in describing the magnificence of the experience.

Oh Shinnah said, "Indeed, you *were* there. This type of rock is found only on one mountain near my people's land. It is both a real and symbolic peak, representing strength and wisdom to the Apaches. The young men, as a test of manhood, had to run four miles holding water in their mouths. The last part of the run was uphill to the summit, a grueling test. If, in their terrible thirst they swallowed the water, they had to wait a year before they tried the run again. The peak represented power, wisdom, healing—qualities the people revered."

I dared not interrupt her moving monologue although one important question was still unanswered. Her eyes closed as she told of her empathy for the troubled times the Apaches had faced since the fall of Cochise. She paused, opened her eyes, looked at me and said, "The name of the magic place on the mountaintop—the name of the stone you held is... 'The Rock of the Healing Waters.'"

In that moment I felt united with her and her people. My empty hand reverberated to its echoes, their talisman, and I still felt imbued with some residue of its potency.

I left the hotel at midnight, floating on a cloud of well-being, and aware that I was in a dangerous section of town for walking alone to my car.

I was relieved to get home and was still high from the evening. Larry was sound asleep but Denny was awake, half-heartedly studying for a test. I desperately needed to tell someone of my extraordinary evening. She listened through her yawns, but needed to finish her work and get to bed.

I was still excited and much too wide awake to fall asleep. Larry was lying on one side, his arthritic back and hips bare and available to my touch. I was vibrating with the night's energy; my hands were pulsing and hot. I laid one hand very gently on his spine, attempting to send him some heat and yet not awaken him. Perhaps I could ease his chronic stiffness.

I watched in total disbelief as my hand appeared to go through his body as though it were not solid flesh. I tried again to put my hand on his back; it passed through as though he were transparent. But he was there: I could see him, feel the heat of my hand, the cooler temperature of his skin—and still his body offered no resistance of skin, bone or muscle. My hand came to rest on the sheet beneath him.

The very strangeness of the physical sensations was accompanied by an inner voice that told me I didn't need to prove anything: since I had held the Rock of the Healing Waters, I *knew* nothing was beyond reach.

I began to tremble, wrapped myself in an extra blanket, and eventually fell asleep.

When Larry awoke in the morning, he stretched, got up, and said, "How was your class last night? I didn't hear you come in, but I have this funny feeling you did something to my back. I feel wonderful—I'm not stiff at all, and I haven't been this limber in years."

I had no idea what had actually happened.

Much as I tried to recapture the healing state that allowed this marvel to occur, I could not. His morning aches returned two days later.

A piece of the Rock of the Healing Waters remained with me. By becoming very centered and quiet—sensing with an inner eye—I could recapture a fragment of its serenity and bliss for a fleeting moment. More important was the awareness that it wasn't related to my ego's need to prove anything. I had been stretched to accommodate a larger view of the potential for human expansion.

Brugh

It seemed much more than coincidence when, in a one-week period in February, 1978, three people who didn't know one another each mentioned to me that I should make every effort to hear a man named Brugh Joy—a physician, a healer and a philosopher who seemed to have an extraordinary ability to expand the lives he touched. He had a ranch in the high desert country near Apple Valley, California, where he held seminars; he was also a frequent speaker at various holistic conferences.

Larry and I had determined that we needed to share more of each other's interests now that the girls were gone, so he agreed to give up his Saturday golf game to hear Dr. Joy speak at Immaculate Heart College in Los Angeles. Other interesting speakers on the two-day program included Buckminster Fuller, Sister Corita Kent, Swami Satchidananda, and Dr. Paul Brenner.

When Saturday came, however, we were both less than enthusiastic about going: I was recovering from the flu that had me bedridden earlier in the week, and Larry had a grudging look in his eyes as he envisioned how wonderful his golf game would be if he hadn't agreed in a moment of weakness to attend the conference. But we'd made a commitment;

neither wanted to be the one to spoil it, and we decided to see if the first day was interesting before making a final decision about Sunday.

Dr. Brugh Joy was not what I expected. He wore a conservative, three-piece suit, more appropriate to his role as a physician than the rebel against traditional medicine he had become. He was above average height, slim, blond, very pale, and he began speaking in a quiet, low voice—not the charismatic wonder I'd heard about.

His story was fascinating, and his manner of speaking was simple, making the facts of his life all the more impressive. Brugh was thirty-nine; he had been Phi Beta Kappa as an undergraduate at U.S.C., graduated from their medical school in the honor society, interned at Johns Hopkins and taken his residency at the Mayo Clinic. He had begun a very successful medical practice in Los Angeles as an internist specializing in lung and heart disease, and was a Fellow in the American College of Physicians.

Four years ago, in January of 1974, his life seemed well on the way of the American dream: a highly regarded profession he enjoyed, a lovely wife, and financial rewards after the many years of study and preparation.

Several months before his thirty-fifth birthday, he began to feel severe abdominal pains that came and went in a pattern. After several months of cyclic pain, the attacks were more frequent—about three weeks apart.

A specialist in gastrointestinal disorders confirmed Brugh's suspicions, and concluded that he had chronic relapsing pancreatitis, an unpredictable disease which can stop for a period of time or progress to a deadly form which has 80% mortality. Commonly, it would lead neither to cure nor death, but many problems due to pancreatic insufficiency.

He could not understand why he would manifest such a disease, and neither his meditations nor personal psychological probes could account for the increasing tempo of the attacks, now occurring every three days. He honored a voice he called the Inner Teacher, but that, too, had no answers.

One Saturday, working on some charts in his office, he felt an incredibly strong urge to enter into meditation and was drawn into a heightened state of awareness which directed him to leave medicine and begin an even deeper course of dedication, involving alternative healing processes and insights which would meld both Eastern and Western thought. The directive was so overpowering he could not doubt it.

Six weeks later, he was on his way and realized for the first time that he'd been pain-free since making his momentous decision. His journeys took him around the world in nine months of travel, study and meditation.

When he returned, he was a changed soul. A vast new world of potentialities had opened and altered him.

Brugh spoke in a rational yet moving way; we felt his disbelief at the possibility of his death at such a young age, the pain of his decision, and the profound joy of his new direction. It was inspiring, but I wondered about his wife, and how she had taken his bombshell decision. He hadn't mentioned whether or not they had children; did he leave them, too?

"I could really enjoy studying with him," Larry said in an enthusiastic voice, and we immediately made plans to attend a conference that Brugh would lead at his ranch, Sky Hi, in two months. It was only three days long, but Larry, always besieged with business problems, felt that he could never get away for the two-week seminars Brugh usually conducted.

We'd no sooner sent in our deposit than Larry had to cancel; an important business convention was planned for the very weekend we were to be at the ranch. I knew the importance of the meeting, but I was very disappointed that again, business always came first.

I really wanted to go. I said, "Well, I guess I'll go alone. I've got to see what's so wonderful about Brugh." In spite of my strong words, I really didn't want to attend by myself, and I felt the cutting edge of resentment toward Larry for not having my commitment to shared experiences like this. Although I didn't play golf, I'd accompanied him on dozens of golfing excursions; I rarely asked him to join me to do things that might not interest him.

In late March, Larry learned he didn't have to be at his out-of-state meeting after all, but now when we called to change the reservation, the ranch was booked and there was a waiting list. Since they only accommodated twenty-four guests, it was unlikely he'd get to go. I wavered, but kept my reservation. I felt like a yo-yo: should I stay home with him or go alone to something that held out the promise of being very special? My pulling and pushing made me realize that I wasn't making a casual decision about a weekend—I needed to come to terms with many of the feelings in my life: how could I reconcile my dependency on Larry and a need to go in my own directions when it conflicted with his plans?

The next day the phone rang. A cheerful voice said, ''This is Sky Hi Ranch, and you and your husband are going to be roommates!'' I was delighted and Larry said he really was looking forward to going.

Before the conference, I had an overwhelming and quite inexplicable urge to send my favorite flower photograph that had appeared in the *Los Angeles Times* to one of the friends who had mentioned Brugh Joy to me. I thought it one of the best things I'd shot, although I'd not sold any prints of it while selling other reproductions of my work. I didn't have my friend's new out-of-state address, and didn't expect to hear from her until Christmas; however, I took the transparency to the printer and ordered a large picture for her. When I picked up the photograph three days later, I came home to find an unanticipated note from my friend, giving her new address. Everything seemed to be fitting so neatly; I mailed the photo in a flurry of optimistic feelings that Brugh Joy and the ranch were going to be very special in my life.

When Larry came home from a brief business trip the night before we were to leave, he was in no condition to go anywhere; he had bent over to pick up his suitcase at the airport and his back had gone into a spasm of pain. He could barely walk.

He took pills for the pain. I did the packing and driving, and we left on Thursday under cloudy, dismal skies that promised to bring still more rain to cap off the rainiest winter ever recorded in Los Angeles.

The conversation reflected the weather and his misery. It was a surprising few hours for me; in our nearly twenty-five years of marriage, he'd rarely been negative about anything, tending to hide whatever emotions he was feeling under a beaming smile and reassuring words. Although I wanted to share everything with him, I was often unaware of the extent of the pressures in his life. He, most certainly, always knew the full range of my moods. It had seemed wonderful to live with a man who was always 'up,' but lately I'd begun to believe that his physical problems stemmed from the very avoidance of dealing with stress, and the masking of any and all negative emotions.

During the four-hour drive, Larry talked openly about his problems. He was concerned about the recent diagnosis of ankylosing spondylitis—arthritis of the spine; he worried that his excessive travel, overweight and occasional incapacitations like this one (or worse) would make all his business efforts futile. It was like a private monologue, and I let him ramble on, glad he felt like talking and aware that I should listen while refraining from giving advice. My suggestions were seldom implemented. No one can force another to change, I thought, but perhaps something helpful will happen this weekend.

After his ramblings, Larry dozed until we turned off the highway to a small road leading into the low hills toward the ranch. Pinpoints of light in a vast dark space were all that identified it in the distance.

As we approached, the ranch buildings looked small and plain, clustered together in unassuming casualness. We were warmly greeted by a woman on the staff. She directed us to our room, which was in the unit nearest to the main house where we would be eating and meeting. It was fortunate we were so close, for Larry was walking with great difficulty. Although he didn't complain, his grunts were enough to tell me the ride had increased his stiffness.

Our bedroom and bath were furnished with well-worn, '40s-style furniture; there were books clustered around, and the place exuded an air of hospitality. Larry lowered himself carefully onto the bed and pronounced it acceptable to his aching back.

After I unpacked, we walked the few feet to the main house to meet the other guests. Dinner was announced with a clanging bell, and seating was arranged through numbered cue balls that matched a corresponding number by each place setting. We were to pick the balls from a covered basket so that at each meal we'd have random seating.

Brugh, in faded jeans, pale shirt and sweater, sat at one end of the L-shaped table. He was very quiet and looked austere, remote. Paul Brenner, his co-leader, sat at the other end of the table. Dinner was light but very tasty: soup, a large salad packed with raw vegetables, home-made baked cookies, fresh fruit juices, and coffee or tea.

Before we finished eating, Brugh stood up and explained our schedule: we were expected to observe an hour of silence before the 8 a.m. breakfast, because so many people meditated during that hour. Morning meetings would begin at ten in the living room, adjacent to the dining room; there would be a break before lunch, our big meal of the day; dinner was to be at six and evening sessions began at eight. Afternoons were free, and we had total freedom to roam the 560 acres.

Our first meeting after dinner was a revelation in many ways. No one who had been here had mentioned any details—they simply said it was remarkable, wonderful, and..."You MUST go there, Bobbie."

There was a sign instructing us to remove our shoes before entering the living room. When we stepped onto the floor, there was an unusually deep, soft feel to the carpeting. I later learned there were two pads beneath it, making the floor seating wonderfully comfortable. There was no furniture. Around the perimeter of the room were large, fat pillows of different colors and fabrics, to be used as seats and backrests. A huge speaker was placed in each corner, plus an imposing array of sophisticated stereo equipment on shelves behind Brugh, who was seated on a pillow waiting patiently for us to settle down.

There were several paintings on the walls, and I put on my glasses to see them better. My mouth dropped open in shock, and I said to Larry, "Look at that picture! Do you recognize it? I don't believe it!" I pointed to Brugh's right. There, perfectly reproduced in oils, was a large replica of the flower picture I'd sent to my friend two weeks ago. There was no mistaking it for any other flower; it was like looking at a photograph of my child in a stranger's home. Who had done the painting? Why was it here? And what an extraordinary coincidence that the very picture I'd sent a friend who'd urged me to come here should be on the wall to greet me!

"Tell me about this picture," I said to Brugh. "Tell me!" As soon as the words escaped I was sure I was making a fool of myself, for he was obviously waiting to start our meeting and I was delaying him, but I didn't care—I couldn't control my excitement. I had to have my questions answered.

"My sister-in-law, Gloria, painted it from a photograph she loved. The painting is very special to me; it's a lotus," Brugh replied calmly.

"It's *not* a lotus. It's a *camellia!* It's my flower—I mean, my photo," I said possessively. Talk about tactlessness and a poor first impression—here I was, out of control, argumentative, and needing to claim ownership. The first session was getting off to a rocky start.

Brugh said nothing more, but smiled—a thin smile, I thought—and Larry motioned me to sit beside him. The evening began with our holding hands in silence. When we broke the circle after several minutes, Brugh began speaking in a low voice, asking us to lie on the floor in a comfortable position, but with our heads pointing toward the center of the room and away from the speakers. He told us that although the music would be excruciatingly loud at times, it would not damage our hearing; if, however, anyone was truly overpowered, he could cover his ears.

The twenty-four of us, plus Brugh, Paul and Carolyn Conger, an associate of Brugh's, packed the floor like colorful sardines in a carpeted can. There were deep sighs as we settled into the rug, then a moment of static followed by the loudest noise I'd ever heard. It sounded as though a symphony orchestra was announcing the end of the world. I felt as though my body would lift off the floor by the sheer force of the sounds: noise was exploding in the room like shrapnel, the floor was vibrating, and I was sure the glass doors would shatter. My first impulse was to preserve my hearing by covering my ears with my hands and bolt from the room, but I made myself lie still and breathe deeply to calm down; surely this had been done many times before with other groups, and there must be a reason. I pictured Brugh smiling as he looked at our discomfort, somehow immune to the noise and putting us to the test.

As the first shock wave subsided, terrifying thoughts flooded my mind, so numerous and so vivid I felt under attack by waves of images tumbling over one another too rapidly to be separated. I fought to unclench my hands that were tingling from the floor, battled to calm myself and relax. The loudness began to diminish, and as it did, I felt less threatened and the imagery slowed. After forty-five minutes of the musical barrage (which included some peaceful passages), I was exhausted, yet in some strange way, refreshed, as though I had been through every emotion and had come out stronger for the contact. My rational mind had been blitzed into submission but deeply buried awarenesses and feelings responded to the sounds.

When the music ended, we returned to sitting positions around the room. Brugh began to speak in a voice that sometimes was below hearing range. Someone asked that he speak louder, and he said, "It does not matter whether you think you can hear me or not. What you need to hear, you will hear."

Then he asked for responses to the music. At first we were hesitant. Then we spoke up, sharing our imagery and discovering that some had felt oppressed by the intensity of the sounds while others had felt a sense of release and freedom. Brugh made a few comments, and occasionally Paul Brenner added his.

When everyone was finished commenting, we joined hands again. It felt different from the first time; we had all been through an experience together, and after the sharing, I could see the outlines of personality beginning to emerge.

We drifted back to our rooms and did little talking before we fell into a deep sleep. I could hardly wait until morning.

We awoke early on Friday. I crawled into Larry's bed for a cuddle, and we snuggled and giggled about the previous night until we remembered we were supposed to be silent. It seemed silly, since we were speaking very quietly, but we decided to honor Brugh's request and see how it felt not to talk. It made me realize that it was a definite plus for our marriage that we were both 'morning people.' Had I been married to a night owl, I would have found it difficult to be energetic in the evening when my system cried out for stillness and a good book; mornings, I needed to share my energy and talkativeness, and someone who needed a long time to get moving would have been driven crazy by my energy.

When Larry got up to shower, he moved very slowly with more than his usual stiffness. I heard the safety cap of the aspirin bottle pop open, a sure sign he was in pain and just one step away from the next medication—a dangerous but effective drug used for inflammation when everything else failed.

As he showered, I opened the front door a few inches to check on the weather, and a blast of cold air swept by me and through the room. It was startlingly clear, and the wind had blown the clouds away.

Larry and I sat apart during breakfast; the billiard ball number had me situated in the middle of the group, away from Brugh and Paul and able to observe both. Brugh was—there was no more appropriate word for it—very Christlike in appearance, very ascetic. His slim body, beard, and piercing blue eyes seemed joined to all the representations of the early religious figures. It was almost as though there was an aura around him which at once attracted people yet bade them keep their distance. My logical mind kept trying to pigeonhole him, but it just didn't work: if I felt he was being distant, then he responded warmly. When I saw him smile, the next time I glanced over he seemed far removed from all of us. He ate little and left quickly while the rest of us continued talking and eating.

Paul Brenner, on the other hand, was open and very demonstrative; the noise level at his end of the table was considerably louder than Brugh's, and filled with easy laughter. Paul was dark haired, tall, very slim and handsome—he looked like a young Rex Harrison. He spoke with animation and listened intently; he was totally involved with whomever he addressed, and I found myself wishing I could hear what was being said and be able to join in the humor.

Our morning session was similar to that of the previous night although the music was different. Sound at intense levels seemed to provoke our deepest fears and wildest joys. Even the timid among us were more talkative, and neither Brugh nor Paul made judgmental comments about any responses.

During lunch, Brugh explained what he wished us to do during our 'free' afternoon. "Find a personal place in which you feel a special harmony; the purity of the natural forces around you will sharpen your awareness, and the silence, plus the absence of telephones, radio, newspapers or television, will accentuate your own perceptions. Prepare for an unexpected teacher, and observe your own inner voice." We were to be "anticipatory and non-demanding in finding this inner teacher." We had the entire 560 acres to roam, and it was entirely possible that we'd see no one else on our walk, for the ranch territory was full of hills and valleys, and to walk it would actually take far more time than one afternoon.

Larry and I were both a little sleepy after lunch and decided to nap before walking. It was always a luxury for him to have the leisure time to relax, although the aspirin must have added to his need to rest. I wanted to be energetic and refreshed for my hike.

We both slept about an hour. Larry awoke with his back hurting more than ever. "I can't walk, honey," he said. "You go ahead. I'm going to take another hot shower and stay in the room."

I put on my warmest sweater and a heavy coat, one that had deep soft pockets to warm my hands and a hood that stayed on my head despite the wind. The wind was like a giant hand pushing me backwards as I climbed the path that wound uphill to the grey-purple hills behind us. I stopped often to rest my legs and catch my breath, wondering if the dark and threatening skies that had crept in since morning were going to pour on us, the tiny creatures struggling in this vast, biblical landscape. I saw other figures far away, but never anyone close enough to tell if the bundled-up forms were male or female.

The cold increased; my nose was running, eyes watering. I kept moving to keep warm. My path wound around a reddish

hill, and I determined that I must get to the top. I felt as though
something wonderful and intensely revealing awaited me
there, and I kept my head down and my feet going. I felt like
a primitive, or a pioneer, on the brink of something unknown,
something inspiring.

I finally reached the top, found a wide rock and plopped
down. I'd lost track of time and the sun gave no clue, for it
was hidden behind dark blue-grey scudding clouds. The rock
offered a convenient spot from which to observe everything—
every blade of grass, every flower and pebble.

Nothing happened. No matter how hard I tried, there was
only me, unenlightened, sitting on a cold rock on a hill in a
chilling wind. I wanted to pretend that it didn't matter, but it
did. I felt I was missing something important that was very
near, something I should have been able to comprehend.

I headed back. It seemed to take forever to get down the
hill and back to the room. I opened the door expecting to see
Larry but he was nowhere to be seen. The furniture was rearranged, and looked as though there was now a room within
a room: chairs had been moved and a suitcase added to make
a rectangle. Suddenly, his dark head poked above the bed
which bordered one side of the cubicle. He turned slowly
toward me with an incredible expression of joy and amazement on his face—a look I'd never seen. He was radiant,
vibrating with some deep emotion, his eyes wide, seeing me
and something else, something not evident to me. He seemed
focused and diffused, all at the same time.

"Darling," he said softly, "Something miraculous is happening to me. I'm not quite through and I need to be alone a
little bit more. Could you go have a cup of coffee, and I'll
come get you in a little while and tell you all about it? I
love you."

I nodded yes, wondering about this new vision of Larry in
ecstasy over...what? I shut the door softly and retreated to
the dining area to warm myself with coffee. I longed for a
drink—preferably a hot toddy, but two or three glasses of
white wine would have done nicely. There was, of course, no
liquor at the ranch, and I felt like a little kid at camp wishing
she could sneak out for forbidden sweets.

There were others around the refreshment area. Most were pleased or excited about their afternoon, eager to talk about their experiences and happy to share the specialness of the day. I was very quiet. I wasn't unhappy—just a trifle lonely and feeling as I had felt so often as a child—different, left out, and missing something wonderful.

Did I always march to a different drummer? When others experienced nothing, I was often intuitive or psychic. But here in this encouraging place that provided time and space for a big leap into the unknown, I seemed grounded, unable to take the next step in developing whatever powers I possessed.

At last, Larry came to the door and motioned for me to come back to the room. I nearly spilled my coffee as I hurried to him, barely able to contain my curiosity a moment longer.

I was not prepared for what he said. Not in my wildest imagination could I have predicted that Larry Probstein— skeptical, logical Larry—would have said, "I've been with dad all afternoon!"

His father had died suddenly of a massive heart attack five and one-half years before. His mother had been devastated by the sudden loss, and Larry, too, was deeply saddened by his father's passing, for they had been warmly appreciative of each other and had worked together until Larry had gone into the insurance business several years earlier.

Nothing in Larry's belief system could account for his description of the afternoon. He did not believe in reincarnation or getting in touch with the dead, but he was awestruck. He was alight with a new glow—wonder, love and delight were all mixed in his voice and eyes. There was no doubt in him as he exclaimed, "He answered all my questions! All the things we talked about on the way up!"

I sat on the edge of the bed and waited for him to continue. A hundred questions were forming in my mind, but I knew I should not interrupt the impassioned description of his experience. He said, "My back was really hurting when you left. After I took a long, hot shower it still hurt, so I decided to see if I could remember how to meditate and relieve some of the pain. I had an urge to make a little area for myself without moving anything very heavy, and I made myself as comfortable as I could get in my little space—I put pillows underneath my neck and knees, took an extra blanket out of the closet to lie on, closed my eyes and tried to relax. But I hurt so much I just couldn't seem to let go. I was just lying there, staring at the ceiling, when dad came to me. He was wearing that old blue sport shirt he loved, and he said he wanted to talk."

"You mean it wasn't a dream? It was really real?" I couldn't restrain myself any longer.

"Well," he laughed joyfully, "We got together in three or four different places, and he was dressed differently each time. We talked about appropriate things in each place."

"Go on, go on."

"The first time, dad and I were sitting in our back yard at the house in his favorite shady spot by the pool. He told me how to change my diet, and what you must buy for me."

"What?" I asked, more curious than ever, for Larry had never expressed much interest in diet. He ate everything that was put before him, no questions asked. He was heavier than he wanted to be by about fifteen pounds. He was a man who ate and drank a lot, downed it quickly and never had a twinge of indigestion or a hangover.

"I have to stop eating red meat," Larry said seriously. "And ice cream and things with flour, too. He said to buy little cans of V8 juice, so I'll drink less booze."

That didn't sound like big news to me. I'd been virtually off red meat for years, and had been trying to talk him into following the same kind of diet. That's just common sense and a repeat of what I've been saying, I thought—it doesn't sound like a big revelation.

But Larry continued as though he were still seeing, touching and hearing his father. "I talked to him again, in our living room. He told me mother will be here for a long time yet, and how I should take care of her.

"The third time was the strangest session of all. It was by far the longest, too. You interrupted me when you came in from your walk, but dad continued on just as though nothing had happened." He smiled at me, "Dad said to give you his love, and told me to tell you that he appreciates all the things you've done for mom.'' He changed position with difficulty and went on, ''Dad came to my office. He was wearing a suit, his favorite bow tie, his New York hat, and he had an overcoat over his arm—you know, as though he had just gotten off the plane and was here for a visit. I realized he'd never been to my new office—he'd never even seen me working in the insurance business. He walked in the door and spoke to the receptionist; he couldn't see me, because I was sitting near the corner of my office, out of his line of vision. I couldn't believe my ears! The secretary said, 'Who may I say is calling?' and dad replied, 'Tell him it's his father.' '' Larry smiled at the warmth of the memory. ''Dad came into my office, put his coat and hat on a chair, and sat down. Then we had a long talk about business. It was really strange—he had no experience in insurance, yet he seemed to know everything I wanted to know. He talked to me about the problems as though he really knew what I've been going through. But the most amazing thing of all was his discussion about my traveling.''

''What? Tell me,'' I urged, hoping that his father advised him to cut back.

''Dad said we shouldn't take that three-week trip in May. I need to take care of things at the office. And he told me exactly what needs attention. He also said the timing is wrong for my trip next week—it just won't work out right.'' Larry was to leave early Monday morning for a 'putting-out-fires' trip of five days. Various accounts were having problems, but none of the accounts were in major cities, and it meant he'd have to spend wasted time waiting for airline connections to each destination.

''Do you think that everything you're telling me really came from your dad?'' I questioned. ''Couldn't it be your subconscious telling you things you feel deep inside but don't express consciously?''

''Dad was here, honey. He really was. I know I wasn't in a trance of any kind. Perhaps some of it was my subconscious, but I'm absolutely convinced that a good part of the information could not have come from me.''

Further questions were cut short by the dinner gong. Larry obviously accepted the reality of his experience; he didn't seem to need to justify it with any theories. It had been an illuminating afternoon: a new world had opened up for him— a world that ran counter to everything he had believed. Would he continue to explore it?

Healers

At breakfast, Brugh announced a change in our morning session. We were going to participate in a healing! I could hardly wait to see for myself what really went on when accomplished healers such as Brugh and Paul set themselves to help someone. I had the highest regard for their intelligence and integrity; I felt their medical credentials and holistic experience made them trustworthy, whereas the television spectacles of faith healers I had inadvertently turned to looked phony and the audience gullible. Here at the ranch I felt I could be a keen, unprejudiced observer. At close range, I could see what happened for myself, and I promised that I'd be as alert and dispassionate as possible.

Brugh told us that a young boy, about ten or eleven years old, would be brought in after our resonation and music. "I want you to know the circumstances of his disability. John is the son of a worker here at the ranch. His hand was nearly severed in a freak accident with an electric saw which was operated by the boy's stepfather, with whom he'd not been on good terms. Physical damage was severe—there is little use of his fingers. Emotional damage was extensive, too."

I certainly didn't expect a physical injury of this type. I'd heard that Brugh had treated people with cancer, and that the subjects had often gone into remission for varying periods of time. Brugh made no claims of any kind, although his reputation as an amazing healer was spreading. But what could he do with a severed wrist, where nerves, tendons and ligaments must have been radically damaged? How could that be helped months after the accident?

Brugh set the ground rules for the healing procedure: ''Paul and I will do our part first. John may have one of two responses to the energy we'll be focusing. He may lapse into a deep, deep sleep or he may go into convulsions that could startle you. Don't be frightened... either response is normal. But do be aware of the highly charged energy field around the table, and lean into it when you approach. I've seen strong men knocked over by the intensity of the field.''

That sounded a bit absurd to me, but then I'd never been around anything like this. Five years ago I would have laughed it off and poked fun at the whole procedure; now I was skeptical but eager to see what would happen. I envisioned John after the healing saying, ''I can use my hand again!'' in a voice full of ecstasy, and all of us weeping tears of joy. I knew this was improbable—it was what I wanted to see but not what would be likely to happen. Still, so many amazing surprises in the metaphysical realm had popped into my life lately, I could no longer say miracles weren't possible.

Brugh continued, ''When you reach the table, you may lay your hands on John anywhere except his head. Do not talk at any time. Take as much time as you feel you need; if I think it's too long, I'll nod to you. When Paul and I are through, we'll go around the circle in order, beginning at my left.''

The morning session began, as usual, with our hands joined; it was a moment of silent devotion that I'd begun to thoroughly enjoy. The warmth and good feelings it engendered went far deeper than words, and the physical contact with whoever was on each side set the tone for the deepening process that lay ahead.

The music at this session was low, primitive, pulsing. It was hypnotic; quiet seemed to penetrate my bones. After it was over and we'd moved to the large pillows, Brugh brought the boy in. John appeared to be very shy. He did not look at us, but sat with eyes cast down as Brugh explained to him what we'd be doing. He gently reached over and picked up John's injured hand. "What use do you have of your fingers?" he asked. John could barely move them at all.

A padded table was brought in and placed in the center of the room. Brugh, Paul and John got up, and the two men helped the boy onto the table. The music began again—the same pulsing beat, the same hypnotic rhythm. Brugh stood at John's head, Paul at his feet. They waited quietly for a few moments, not touching him, and evidently centering and preparing themselves for the task ahead.

With utmost gentleness, they began to lay their hands on the boy. He sighed deeply and appeared to go into a deep sleep immediately, unaware of the two men. As they circled him, their movements were as intertwined as a *pas de deux;* they seemed more like dancers joined in harmony to an unheard symphony than healers attempting to renew a wounded boy. They were always in balance at either end of the table or at either side of John, yet with eyes closed they seemed oblivious of each other.

The silence, other than the steady, low pulsing of the music, seemed palpable, the air thicker. No one moved at all, not even slight posture adjustments to ease backs or knees. I wondered if I were the only one who was miserable. I'd suddenly begun to have what felt like menstrual cramps, although I wasn't expecting my period; worse, I desperately had to urinate, and the insistent pressure was getting stronger and stronger. I regretted having had the second cup of coffee for breakfast, but I dared not leave and break the intense mood in the room.

I lost all track of time. The music beat on and on as my body ached and cramped.

I felt a slight nudge in my ribs from Larry, who motioned with his head to look at Paul.

Something was wrong. He was holding each of John's ankles, but Paul's knees were buckling and his head was sinking lower to his chest. He was a slow-motion picture of a man passing out. Suddenly Carolyn and Jack, a member of our group, eased to their feet and moved quickly to support Paul and lead him back to his seat. Paul didn't seem to know where he was. Carolyn took his place. Brugh didn't appear to have noticed; he still maintained an unmoving stance at John's head with his eyes closed.

At last he nodded to Nancy, the first person in the circle; she walked slowly to the table and began to touch John very gently on the wrist.

I was near the end of the group. My pains alternated with a profound sense of the beauty of this tableau: John seemed to be in absolute peace, and each participant tenderly and respectfully touched him while Brugh maintained his hands at the boy's head. Nothing visible was happening. I did not know what I would do.

I walked to the table, wishing I were less conscious of the pains in my body and more suffused with a sense of healing ability. I wasn't aware of the field of energy as I neared Brugh, John and Carolyn, yet something slowed me down. Time seemed to be passing in a slower way. I felt as though I were walking just slightly above the ground, but none of this seemed unusual or in any way special—it was all rather like watching a movie of myself. I didn't feel any great compassion for the boy as I touched him, nor did I feel removed. My pains stopped. I put my left hand gently on his chest and my right hand at his wrist. My hands moved, my eyes took in Brugh and Carolyn and the body beneath me, but no more. I felt neither powerful nor helpless, as though my emotions, in addition to time, had been suspended.

Then I turned to leave the table, and once again sharp cramps assailed me, bringing me back to awareness of the room and making me wish I could run to the bathroom and come back without being noticed.

Larry was laying his hands on John now, a look of exquisite tenderness on his face. I imagined him visualizing John as the son we'd never had, and I made a mental note to ask him later if this was so.

When each of us had taken our turn, Brugh gently woke the boy and led him to a pillow near his own. He asked in a very low, quiet voice, "How do you feel?"

John was unaware of us and unable to respond coherently, as though he'd been aroused in the middle of the night and was still asleep. Brugh didn't press him further. John did not use his hand, but neither was he actively moving any other part of his body. I felt disappointed that I couldn't see any change. Our meeting broke up shortly afterwards and I ran to the bathroom.

I was anxious to talk to Larry. I had very ambivalent feelings about the whole morning. I was attracted by the music and the intensity of Brugh, Paul and Carolyn, but I was hesitant to admit that anything had really been altered. It was mystifying; I wanted a conclusive result, like the chemistry experiments I'd done in high school. Perhaps we'd hear more later, for I imagined Brugh would talk about it.

I returned to the meeting room to find Larry talking to a man and woman, who, by their dinner conversation the night before, were both in healing professions. Everyone had left but the four of us. The table was still in the middle of the room. I interrupted their conversation when I said, "I wish we could all do something to help Larry's back pain." I knew he wouldn't have said anything, and I felt this was the perfect moment to help him without interfering with Brugh's schedule.

"I'd love to," Nancy said, getting to her feet at once and pulling her friend up. "Dick, stand at Larry's head, Bobbie at his feet, and I'll work on his back."

"Shall I lie on my stomach?" Larry asked. He added playfully, "Or do your healing rays go all the way through if I lie on my back?" I noticed he didn't describe the pain.

"Lie on your stomach, silly," Nancy giggled.

I'd long wondered if I could learn enough about healing to focus whatever abilities I had to permanently help him. I wanted to heal him! I desperately wanted to do something—anything—rather than watch silently as he suffered the chronic stiffness and occasional intense flare-ups of pain. He rarely complained, but I knew his silence often masked fear he was reluctant to reveal.

I placed my hands on Larry's feet. I felt as though I were a child making a mighty wish for a dream to come true. I willed something extraordinary to happen. I felt our love could conquer anything; certainly his pain must succumb to such blazing power!

I looked up at Dick just before the wave of nausea hit me and the room began to spin. Pains stabbed me in my lower abdomen, and, like Paul, I began to sink toward the ground; unlike Paul, I wasn't in a trance. I let go of Larry's feet as though they were hot potatoes and rushed out of the room and back to our bathroom, where I threw up.

Nothing in this weekend was as I expected it to be. I never had menstrual pains, and I rarely threw up. Exhausted, I lay down on my bed and tried to figure out what possibly could have happened. Perhaps if I breathed slowly and deeply I could relax and let go of discomfort, but I took two aspirin to help me along the way.

Fifteen minutes later Larry burst through the door. "I can't believe it! The pain is gone! Nancy laid her hands on my back, I felt blazing heat, and after a few minutes, the pain disappeared! It's gone—really gone! Look—I can move now—and no pills ever worked that fast!" He pirouetted around the room, grinning like a kid at Christmas.

"But what happened to you?" he said. "One minute you were there and the next minute you'd gone."

After lunch, I asked Nancy and Dick what they'd observed.

Dick said, "You and Larry have a special radiance—a rare chemistry together that's very beautiful. But when you went to lay your hands on him, your emotional attachment got in the way. Instead of just allowing yourself to be an energy channel, you permitted yourself to be drained. That's why Brugh has stressed unconditional love."

Nancy added, "I'll bet you were *demanding* that Larry be healed. You can't do that. You have to protect yourself—let the energy flow *through* you. Most of all, you must let *his* body use the energy any way it needs to. You wanted to use the energy *your* way, and that's *not* the way it works."

Dick said, "I could see you beginning to wobble when you put your hands on his feet. I tried to signal you."

Nancy said, "I could feel the energy at your end just fizzling out. But you look fine now, and maybe it was a good lesson for you."

That day, I learned never to touch anyone when I was not feeling up to par. Not only was I unable to help another, but I became a soggy, wet sponge...absorbing negative energy instead of channeling a positive force.

Brugh's discussion of unconditional love, however, was a lesson I was not ready to integrate. He had said, "unconditional love is not mental, emotional or sexual; it is an awareness of universal values and relationships that allows one to sense the deepest unity in everything. It is not judgmental and not selective: it embraces life as a whole."

While the theory sounded terrific, it seemed an impossible dream to me. If he did exemplify unconditional love, then I found it a little cold in actual practice. Well, I thought, maybe I'm just not ready for all this healing and universal love. Maybe I just don't have what it takes—perhaps I'm just too emotionally filled with fears and loves and doubts.

The luck of the seating system at lunch brought me next to Paul Brenner. Despite the morning's problems, he was talkative and bright. "I don't recall anything after people tell me I started to crumple. I don't even remember being helped to my pillow. That's never happened to me, although I've worked with Brugh before. But he's a very powerful man and maintains an amazing energy level."

"What happened to John's wrist? Is it better?"

"I don't know," Paul answered. "And...it doesn't matter."

"Why not?" I asked, rather sharply. How could they not care whether or not their efforts had any impact?

"It doesn't matter. If you get hung up with ego gratification in healing, and if you demand results, you'll be defeated before you start. You are a channel of energy. The body you're working with may use that force in any way it needs, and it may well not be the way you assumed. Healing may not be visible, and it may not show immediate results."

"You mean... 'sometimes the magic works, and sometimes it doesn't?'"

"It may work in ways that are not apparent to you," Paul replied with a smile.

No wonder scientists throw their hands up in dismay at the healing arts! Not only are positive results sporadic, but the healer isn't supposed to demand results! If detachment is essential, does that mean not caring? I had assumed that loving and caring were prerequisites. The idea that I could disengage my emotions when working with Larry or any deeply loved person was new and sounded impossible—for me, at least. But Paul was persuasive, and I could certainly see the advantage to being less emotionally involved. The lesson had been well taught just an hour before, but the day was so full of newness that I couldn't assimilate everything, and, rather than argue or sound slow-witted, I changed the subject.

Paul spoke often and lovingly of his wife and children, and mentioned that he, like Brugh, had left medicine to follow his heart's lead into holistic pursuits. Unlike Brugh, he hadn't disengaged from the deep relationships in his life. He'd left only his practice of obstetrics; his ex-partners thought he was crazy to leave a prosperous partnership for a dream, but he seemed delighted with his choice.

I hated to end the conversation, but the room had emptied and Paul wanted to rest. I, too, wanted to lie down and talk to Larry about this amazing day.

He was still free of pain. We lay on our beds and talked. He was thoroughly enjoying himself and was delighted he had come; a whole new world had opened to him: the prospect of life without aches and pains, and a continuing dialogue with his father. His body was suddenly free and his mind was challenged by Brugh and Paul.

I was finding surprises at every turn—not all of them delightful—and I wanted something wonderful to come along, grab me by my ears and lift me above my doubts...elevate me to a fantastic, transcendental experience. What was the next step for me on my stumbling pathway of psychic awareness and healing practices? Was I demanding too much and giving too little? Not seeing immediate results was difficult for me to accept. I set up MY expectations and assumed they would be met. Was I doing that with everything in my life?

"This is so much MORE than I ever expected," Larry exclaimed joyfully. "Thank you, darling, for being interested in all this. I'm so glad I'm here!"

We talked and talked, then finally napped for half an hour. When I awoke, I was feeling much better and decided to go for a hike. Larry wanted to read a bit, then wander around the lower areas of the ranch where walking wouldn't be strenuous.

We kissed goodbye. I laced up my hiking boots, zipped up the coat, opened the door and headed out into a world that felt new and pure. Last night's heavy rain had disappeared into the harsh desert soil. Flowers were bursting into bloom everywhere, and their fragrance mingled with the clear fresh breeze blowing from the hills. There was a lightness in the air, a fullness of color and scent, a richness of shapes and forms of flowers. I felt as though I had never truly breathed before this day, before this moment.

I walked effortlessly, stopping occasionally to touch or pick a flower and listen to the insects humming. Mauves and grey-greens, hot pinks and bright yellows dotted the desert landscape and blended harmoniously with decaying vegetation and brown rocks.

One of the ranch dogs loped near me, making forays into the sagebrush and returning to the path where I walked. I enjoyed watching him; I was in no hurry to get anywhere, and wandered slowly uphill, eyes more on the ground than on the hills ahead. I felt no push to become enlightened; it seemed more than good enough just to be alive and to be here, walking, touching, seeing, smelling, sensing the springtime rhythms of the desert.

I found myself near a water storage tank I had noticed the day before. It seemed a strange object, and I circled it, walking a little above and beyond to get a better perspective. The round white top, perhaps fifteen feet in diameter, was paved with an abrasive coating that looked like very rough sandpaper; from a short distance away it appeared to be a giant sparkling drum. The weathered wooden supports that braced it merged into the underbrush.

Suddenly I was excited and felt drawn to the tank. I needed to stand on its roughness, feel protected by the perfect circumference of its rim. I climbed up, discarding my coat but taking the tiny, wilting flowers I'd put in my linty pockets. I put the flowers down carefully near the tank's edge.

Somehow, I knew it was important to sit in the exact center of the drum facing west. I sat cross-legged, the circle drawn around me, its glittering texture sharply contrasted against the muted tones of the desert. It seemed appropriate and somehow very comforting to place myself at the center of a small universe and know I could move freely from the center in any direction I might choose. The distance was not important. I was at peace—protected yet free.

Time had no meaning. I felt a part of the glory of the day. I stood up and stretched my entire body upwards, wiggling my fingertips at the sky; I envisioned myself as a small link between heaven and earth. Welling up inside me was an urge to do a kind of dance—a ritual dance—as though I were an Indian honoring the elements. First I bowed to the west and east, then north and south. I began to sway and move in a small circle in the center of the drum, hearing my booted feet tap out a rhythm on the gravelly surface. A voice suddenly poured out of me in a tuneless song of time and space, in no language but in deep, reverberating tones. I circled the tank, still singing, moving around the lip to the right, then back to the left.

I saw something shining dully near the edge; I bent to pick up a nail. It seemed important—worthy of some deep attention. How had it found its way to me? I picked up my drooping flowers too, and sat down once more, slightly out of breath and feeling happily centered. It was as though my being were in a smaller, denser body with a mind that encompassed vast knowledge.

It was necessary to contemplate these symbols in my open hands. The nail was pointed, direct, firm, probing. The flowers, soft and malleable, were limp yet still full of scent and resiliency. Each hand held the opposite of what lay in the other palm; each was somehow a balance to the other in a deeper sense than texture and form, density and color.

The knowledge flooded upon me and echoed through my bones that I'd always delineated my world in terms that excluded seeing both sides simultaneously; something was either good *or* bad, right *or* wrong, dark *or* light. But at this moment, the world seemed limitless, composed of both opposites and innumerable mid-points that were all aspects of a mutable reality. The nail could bind two parts together, drive them apart, or lie inert until needed, its sharpness and firmness unused. The pliant flowers could engulf the structure that nails and wood and metal had formed, or break through concrete as weeds broke through the rigidity of man-made forms, or they could bloom and fade into the soil, unnoticed.

All of us seem bent upon defining and destroying, explaining and erecting monuments to ourselves, our ideas, our relationships. It all appeared so insignificant and—most of all—so very transitory, unnecessary: the world IS. To be in harmony with it means to take all of it in and let all of it out, like a slow easy breath that maintains life but must be expelled to allow another to come in. Had all the strivings of mankind done any good? What was, WAS, and all the justifications and explanations were futile. In this timeless moment, I felt no need to understand 'why' things were so unfair, or 'why' war and disease took their merciless toll of innocent people. It no longer seemed important to understand the unknowable answers to very human questions. I would rather be fully aware of health as well as sickness, birth as well as death, and joyfulness in an often turbulent world.

There was peace within me as I understood that this was all I needed to know. Since I could not change the world, perhaps I had best become more a part of it...be more accepting, less demanding—and in that process, more loving.

The sky had begun to redden and glow. The air was cooling quickly. I saw several people walking down from the hills; they were moving specks against a violet background. I no longer felt content to be here alone within my circle; I wanted Larry's arms about me, his body next to mine.

I climbed down carefully, holding the nail and the flowers, got into my coat and walked quickly back to our room.

At our evening session, Brugh seemed very warm as well as wise. I found myself responding to him in a new way and able to absorb more of what he said without resisting it. Had I changed, or had he? Was he just a reflection of my own feelings about myself? I felt as though I'd come a long way since the first night.

Larry left early to read in bed and I lingered in the dining area, drinking coffee and eating cookies. Paul Brenner was talking to a small group of people who were discussing astrology. As they drifted away, I moved over to talk to him.

He reminded me so much of Larry, even though they didn't sound or look alike.

"You really believe in astrology?" I asked in surprise, for I didn't see how intelligent people could believe that stars influenced behavior on earth; more, I thought that people born on the same day would always have different tendencies because their heredity was singular.

"Astrology has a great deal of validity," he said. "My birthday is in May, and I'm strongly a Gemini, with some Taurus traits thrown in."

My heart was beating strangely. "When's your birthday?"

"May 21."

"That's Larry's birthday too! What a coincidence!"

Paul was delighted. He added, "You know, you remind me so much of my wife, Joyce. You two don't look alike, but your mannerisms and responses are much the same."

"Oh, I'm one of those lovable Virgos," I said, not really knowing what a Virgo was supposed to be. "I've been told by people who think they know astrology that my tendencies toward perfectionism are a dead give-away."

Now it was Paul's face that changed expression. "When's your birthday?"

"September 10."

"I don't believe it!" He smacked the palm of his hand to his forehead. "That's incredible! You and Joyce have the same birthday too! That's the first time that's ever happened to us!"

We laughed and shared stories of our spouses' idiosyncrasies, resolved to get the four of us together and certain we would have a lot of fun when we did.

The next morning Larry and I waited for breakfast in the sunshine on the terrace. The weather had warmed considerably and the desert was bursting with new life.

I'd brought a blank book to the ranch, thinking I would do a great deal of writing. So far, I had written nothing. Lazily, I opened the book and gazed into the distance; my hand, resting on the page, began to write firmly and in great haste:

> There is a simultaneity of positive and negative and the fulcrum for you to balance both is merely the observation that both do operate at all times for all people in all circumstances and that this is all right and needs no further explanation or resolution. This is the open secret. This is 'the answer'.....and in this is the resolution of polarities. Take a new silence now to expand the listening and you will feel less need to talk to fill spaces.
>
> More! Less is more and less is still immeasurable..... forget not thy nail and thy flower.

The breakfast bell rang and we all trooped in. I put the book next to me against the chair leg. No one had seen what I'd written, and I didn't feel it was necessarily from Paul, my guide. It was, after all, a different version of what I'd experienced on the water tank.

I was stunned when Brugh looked at me and said, "It's important for you to keep your life in balance. Look in the corner of the room, and notice the scale I keep there. It's a symbol of the polarities of life, always balanced by the fulcrum. You must be aware of yourself as that center, that fulcrum, and return to your center when you feel out of balance." I nodded, then said in surprise, "But that's what I wrote in my book a little while ago!" Brugh smiled and said nothing more.

I wasn't sure if Brugh even knew my name, but he certainly was able to sense into my mind; many of the people in our group had mentioned that he had a remarkable ability to express their deepest, unspoken thoughts.

After the morning session I told Paul about my automatic writing, which still puzzled me. "Why me, Paul? Why this writing, especially at this time in my life when I wasn't interested in any of this a few years ago? What's the point?"

Paul grinned and replied, "Maybe you're in *training*, Bobbie. Have you thought of that? How long have you been doing this?"

"About six or seven years."

"That's not much time, is it?"

"I guess not." I hadn't thought of it that way. "I never think of how far I've come—only how far I have to go." His idea sounded strange; perhaps I *WAS* in a new school—a kindergarten of an altered reality—and learning a new alphabet of relativity. Perhaps I was also unlearning time and space definitions I had assumed were unbending. The more I thought about Brugh's insistence that none of us had even begun to experience the magnificence of our possibilities, the more it made sense.

Home

We left the ranch late Sunday afternoon. Larry was still pain-free and basking in the memory of his afternoon with his father. I enjoyed renewed energy and a sense of peace with the world.

We'd taken names and addresses of other participants and promised to get together; I had discovered that Nancy, the healer who had worked so well on Larry's back, lived near us. The ideas that Brugh and Paul had presented were exhilarating, and I resolved to explore some of them in my own meditation and reading. Above all, I realized we had been given a great gift: an awareness, at an individual level, of the incredible potential of the human race.

Our trip home was the antithesis of the journey to the ranch; less than four days had passed, yet we each felt we were not the same. But had we truly changed? Would the glow from our experiences alter us...deepen us...or would it fade as we slipped back into the mainstream of our lives?

An interesting surprise awaited us at home: each of four messages on our answering machine was to cancel a stop on Larry's trip. His father had been right...the timing was wrong. None of the calls had been related and Larry was impressed!

After the casualness of the ranch, our living-dining room looked so formal and rigid I planned to sell our two stiff sofas and the large glass coffee table to make our home a comfortable place of repose.

I found a pair of double-width reclining chaises that were exactly what I wanted, but Larry said, "How will I know if they're good for my back?"

"Well, you'll just have to come to the store to test them." Larry never found time to shop for anything; he always professed to love whatever I bought, and much preferred business and golf to shopping for clothes or furniture.

"How will I know they're good support?" he insisted. He usually wasn't argumentative. I decided not to tell him our old furniture was being picked up the following week.

When we got to the store, he sank awkwardly onto the curved surface with a grimace. It quickly changed to a grin. "I don't believe it!" he said, "Howard! How the hell are you?"

"Great, Larry. What are you doing here in the middle of Bullock's curled up in that wonderful chair?"

Larry introduced us. Howard was the orthopedic surgeon who had diagnosed his arthritis. The doctor sat on the other chaise and pronounced it ideal for anyone with a back problem. I was thoroughly delighted with the dialogue.

As we left the store after ordering the furniture, Larry said, "I'm becoming a believer. I'm *definitely* becoming a believer!"

For several months after our retreat at Brugh's, life did, indeed, seem easier. Most of the time I was able to suspend my natural inclination to expect things to happen my way and to become irritated or disappointed if they didn't. The very lack of demands opened up a whole new world that was much easier to live in. To my enjoyment, my tendency to be a perfectionist eased away.

Except on rare occasions, 'The Judge'—my critical, nagging inner voice—disappeared. I moved more freely, delighting in each day and the surprises it brought, no longer demanding that it be what I expected.

My life was rich with variety, full of family, new and old friends, photographic assignments and other interesting projects. In the past, I was a juggler, afraid to drop anything, but unable to stop the endless movement. Now, somehow, I had more energy, more time, and was able to do it all, gliding easily into rest or meditation as well as activity.

Still, Brugh's 'unconditional love' remained an unattainable goal and a catchy phrase. After all, I knew very well I couldn't convert instantly to his basic philosophy. I looked at my Sky Hi nail and the remains of my flowers nearly every day as a reminder of the necessity to balance myself.

I didn't consider myself 'enlightened.' I was an amateur healer. I didn't want to be a teacher. If all these potentials were in me, an inner wisdom knew it was not time to come into their flowering; I knew I wasn't ready to assume any of the responsibilities that went with them.

Friends were curious about our experiences at the ranch, but I had little to say and the profound experience on the drum was too personal to be discussed. Larry was more than willing to discuss his 'happening.' Some quickly changed the subject or became uncomfortably silent when Larry spoke of the dialogues with his father. They didn't think he was lying, but their experiences could neither accept nor process such information. Years before, I would have reacted the same way.

Stories of my psychic happenings over the last several years had provoked casual interest. Psychic phenomena, apparently, were far easier to ignore than deal with. At first I was surprised that discussions rarely went beyond a superficial level, but I learned not to challenge. If people were genuinely interested in the ramifications of psychic phenomena, they asked. When they didn't, they were usually not prepared to listen with an open mind. I understood—it took intense effort to open doors that culture and education had sealed off. Anything that attacked science and medicine was threatening, since it undermined established belief systems.

Only the topic of healing prompted undivided attention. After all, everyone had a pain, a condition, a disease. Few wished to take responsibility for what their bodies told them. Only during talks about healing did I sense a tremendous surge of curiosity and genuine willingness to accept that the rational mind and traditional medicine might *not* have all the answers. When Larry told of his pain relief through the laying-on of hands, friends literally sat forward in their seats, intent on every word. The very fact that they knew him to be so logical lent credence to his words.

Larry didn't dwell on any of the paranormal events as I did. He was neither beguiled by their mystery nor seduced by their novelty. The same couldn't always be said for me.

I became aware that Larry and I were a small bridge between two worlds. We were traditionalists in our values and life style, and couldn't be discounted as long-haired dreamers existing on the fringe of society. We often shocked and provoked people, but we always intrigued them. Many asked for recommendations of books to read, classes to attend. My ever-expanding library was always open, and I loved to share books and pass on information about seminars and programs.

Students have a way of moving from 'guru' to 'guru' seeking answers to eternal questions. They often attach and detach quickly, glorifying or demeaning their teachers as though they are comparing products instead of people. Some leaders in the human potential movement had fallen into enormous ego trips, exploiting trusting students—no different from any field, for they were merely human, after all. I remained conscious of my need to avoid slavish devotion to any teacher, even as I enjoyed their exceptional gifts.

Brugh had done his best to dissuade anyone from looking to him as a 'guru,' although some very overt attempts had been made. Would he always be able to resist those pressures? Perhaps the intense commitment to his inner teachers and long hours of meditation would continue to stabilize his life, no matter how famous he might become.

Although I was aware of a higher path, I too felt myself slowly sliding back to the old ways. I found I could not maintain my inner peace without constant renewal.

Brenner

I stayed in touch with Paul Brenner after the retreat at Sky Hi. Our easy camaraderie and common birthdays encouraged furthering the friendship. Along with another couple—an ex-priest and his delightful wife—Larry and I made a date to visit Paul and Joyce at their La Jolla home.

I happily anticipated a leisurely day with the six of us discussing fascinating ideas. But, as happened so often, Larry changed plans at the last minute to fly east on an urgent business matter. Paul wouldn't have free time again for many weeks so we let the arrangements stand.

My grumpiness at going alone faded as I started the two-and-a-half hour drive down the coast. The air was clear and warm, the hills vibrant with colorful wild flowers, the music from the car stereo especially full and rich. I missed the turnoff and had to retrace my route, but it was a delight rather than an annoyance.

Joyce greeted me at the door. Shining brown hair, simply cut, framed magnificent turquoise eyes and a warm smile. What a marvelous face, I thought, and hoped I'd get a chance to shoot some portraits of her.

121

The Cassidys had just arrived, and we sat on a deck by the pool in the sunshine, sharing ideas and laughter. Joyce was friendly but busy, answering the phone or greeting people who appeared to flow through the house without ever ringing the bell. At lunchtime, she prepared sandwiches and cold drinks. I wondered if she always had to be available as a perennial hostess, since his patients, their friends, children and friends of their children all made the Brenner home a social center. Still, she managed to find bits of time to sit with us. Occasionally there was a guardedness about her that reflected a quality I sensed in myself, and I was curious about her background.

Paul said he'd barely made it into medical school; his grades had been considerably less than outstanding. Yet, once his curiosity was aroused, he did well at his studies, and even managed to study a little law as well as medicine. Now his interests included physics, philosophy, religion, medicine, healing, and teaching. He wore all his gifts lightly, seemingly unaware of his charisma, his obvious attractiveness. Joyce was intelligent, delightful, and a strong personality in her own right, and I felt she buffered the world for Paul to give him the time and space to expand while she took care of all the details. I felt a tinge of envy that she could share so much of his life work and even have people like Elisabeth Kübler-Ross as a houseguest.

I had been with Larry when he displayed Paul's qualities in the business world. I admired Larry's grasp of finance and insurance, and his ability to bring people and ideas together. At times I felt I was married to a lovable computer, and I often listened in amazement to the man I'd married over twenty-five years before, wondering at the transition from an easygoing boyishness to power and strength.

I, too, handled as much as I could, and I felt that Joyce and I probably shared some of the same problems and delights in being married to men who were charismatic and inventive. Their ideas surfaced so quickly that most could never be thoroughly implemented; I had the feeling we were both left tending to details while they were on another project completely, dropping the last. Many times I had felt deprived of

Larry's time and attention because of his consuming passion for business, even though I enjoyed the advantages of traveling and meeting new people through his work. If Joyce had to maintain an 'open house' all the time (which I didn't, since Larry was away on trips so much), she had an extraordinarily busy life.

The Cassidys left early in the afternoon and Joyce excused herself to run errands and attend an exercise class. I sat with Paul, asking questions about some automatic writing I'd brought with me. He suggested we go into the meditation room so I could write for him.

The room was a converted garage, just a few steps from the woodsy pool area where we'd been sitting. It was done beautifully and simply, with rich brown carpeting, pillows in blue tones thrown in the corner, a hanging fireplace suspended in the middle with a brick hearth around it, two huge abstract paintings in flowing colors and a large sliding glass door leading to the pool. A music system, sofa and treatment table completed the room. Posted prominently was a sign reading, "Please—no shoes, food or drink."

I felt a strong twinge in my stomach. After all, Paul was so attuned to the holistic, healing, paranormal world, such a well-known professional, I felt out of my league. He relaxed like a large, denimed pretzel, half-closing his eyes and appeared perfectly happy to be doing nothing.

"Paul," I said hesitantly, "First, I'd like to write whatever comes through—then you can ask questions. OK?"

He nodded yes, eyes heavily lidded and sleepy.

I began to write in large, firm strokes, indicating to me that I was getting definite information from my Source. I lost track of time as I bent over the paper. I felt at peace, yet elated and excited. I read what I'd written to Paul, and he nodded without much expression.

"Paul, ask what you wish."

He asked, "Is there more I should be doing in medicine now?" My hand wrote:

The circle will be completed. There is a definite denial if you press now.....it is done, but not soon.

You will return, but to an expanded field doing inte-
grational work.

It would be easy to assume that Paul missed the obstetrics
he'd practiced for ten years, although he did leave it by his
own choice. I couldn't let my rational processes interfere.
My hand produced a diagram to show that medicine would,
after several years, begin to include some of the healing work
it now scorned; in that context, Paul would return to medicine.

He asked, "As we move in consciousness, does the center
of balance change?"

The Light within is the center and it does not change
.....only the awareness changes. The center is a
radiance which extends outwards.....for you, a cen-
ter is in the fingers, but not here for most—your
fingers see and the heart loves. In a complete being
the body vibrates in harmony and all the end points
are centers as well. There is in this division of ques-
tion and response no separation, as there is no sepa-
ration at the highest levels, for at these points there
is no center, for all IS.

Paul nodded, and said the mention of his hands was accurate, that he'd done diagnostic 'scanning' work through his
fingers that doctors refused to believe. He had been asked to
diagnose a patient who was a complete stranger to him, using
only his scanning methods and extraordinary 'senses,' and
bypassing any traditional tests or examination. A team of doctors then took every test they could think of, using every tool
known to medicine. Paul's analysis was totally accurate. The
doctors could not explain what he'd done and dismissed the
incident as a coincidence. This had happened more than once,
and he finally stopped submitting himself to tests when the
medical men gave no credence to anything he did when he
didn't use medical means to achieve his results.

Paul asked, "Is Christ consciousness the lowest level of the
next pyramid?" I had no idea what he meant, but my hand
wrote energetically:

No. It is the highest level of this one. There is at the
infinite level an awareness of that which is beyond

containment of form and it is not in this plane that
this can be so except in rare cases. The cosmos exists
in rare purity which contains no borders nor defini-
tion because human senses have been outmoded by
a keen sense of ONENESS AS FLUIDITY.

I didn't understand what pyramid levels meant, but I felt that a truth had been written that echoed something unknown yet deeply sensed in me—something long buried beneath layers of education, of training, of rational thought that had never included a radiant center nor oneness as fluidity.

I was confused by 'Christ consciousness.' As a Jew (even if I didn't observe many of the traditions), I found it difficult to embrace, although my metaphysical experiences always showed the *oneness* of profound spiritual belief rather than the separateness fostered by every religious tradition. Paul felt that Christ consciousness meant an individual's relationship to the divine, as manifested through an archetype, or model.

I wrote more, much more. Paul lay propped on an elbow, lost in his own thoughts as I wrote, sometimes looking up to hear my response to another of his questions.

Paul said quietly, "Bobbie, you have a great gift. You really don't need any more teachers. The knowledge you seek is within you—all of it. All you need is the confidence to accept it."

I was overwhelmed with love and gratitude for the guidance I'd received, both inner and outer, and to the Source within me. A new sense of respect for my own internal wisdom surfaced without my usual self-doubts.

Suddenly I was exhausted. "Paul, that's it. I need to rest a while."

He smiled, stretched, and suggested I stay and meditate while he went to make phone calls in the other room.

About twenty minutes later I was somewhat revived; Joyce was home and unpacking groceries. She asked me to stay to dinner and I accepted gladly. I was feeling happy and rather mellow, not looking forward to the drive back to Los Angeles in the evening traffic. I would have loved a glass of wine, but remembered Joyce saying that neither of them drank alcohol or coffee. I wish I could have said that; I'd certainly be healthier without them. Perhaps some day I'd be free of two of my bad habits.

I couldn't help but overhear conversations while I was cleaning vegetables. Paul was treating some very ill people with his own kind of therapy, provided they continued to take whatever medical treatments their doctor had prescribed. He'd had some very positive results, which medicine discounted. He was besieged with offers to speak, to teach, to treat. I thought *our* household was busy... the Brenners could have used a switchboard!

During dinner, I observed Paul with his family. The similarity to Larry continued to amaze me. Perhaps astrology had something to it after all—I had always perceived it as a toy for the ignorant, but my preconceptions in the last few years were like plaster ducks sitting on a wall in an amusement park, waiting to be shot down.

Joyce and I did the dishes after dinner. Paul wandered in and put his arms around her, kissing the back of her neck as she bent over the sink.

"Why not stay the night?" he suggested to me. "We have an extra bedroom."

"Oh, do stay," Joyce added. "I'd love to have you write for me. And it's silly to drive all the way home at night to sleep in an empty house."

I accepted, pleased I had thought to pack a toothbrush and change of clothes in case I tired and chose to spend the night in Laguna. Never had I spent a day like this before—just hanging on and on; still, it felt right to be here, and I realized I'd been hoping they'd ask.

Joyce and I went into the meditation room and curled up on the floor. We needed heat now, for the fog had rolled in from the Pacific, two blocks away, and the evening damp penetrated the glass wall.

I began to write for her, but not with the same strength I had earlier for Paul. As sometimes happened, I was getting trivia. I kept writing:

FAN TASIA

in large letters, underlined and circled heavily. Joyce couldn't
figure out what it meant. Suddenly she looked up and giggled.
"I had an Aunt Phasia I was very close to. Could that be it?"

It certainly was. Information occasionally came through as
a play on words or twisted in some simple way that needed
decoding. The rest of my writing was fairly general, and I was
disappointed at not doing better. At least I was getting to
know Joyce, for we talked between my scribbles. I liked her
more and more.

Paul came in and after hearing my complaint that I wasn't
doing very well, suggested Joyce write for me.

"I haven't ever done it," she said.

"Joyce is really good at psychic things," he said, smiling
down at her. "She just doesn't believe it yet that she IS good."
He bent down to kiss her, and I was warmed by the affection
between them.

I handed Joyce my book, and she began to write for me while
I lay back and closed my eyes. She was quite accurate, and
came up with specific names that were definitely in my life.
I wondered if the ability to write of another's life was in many
of us, latent and unexpressed because it was so rarely used.

As Joyce wrote on, we talked and laughed, the similarities
of our likes and dislikes becoming clearly evident. Our mannerisms, preferences, even our body language seemed familiar
to the other.

When we finally said goodnight, I felt I'd known her for
years—not just for a very long day.

The next morning I awoke at six, feeling rested and alert
although I usually slept later. I decided to go for an invigorat-
ing walk on the beach.

Paul was already up, dressed, and on his way out to meet
someone for an important breakfast get-together. He offered
to drive me to the beach and I accepted.

"I'm usually out surfing by now," he said.

The image of this lanky, long-haired, forty-ish ex-physician
cruising to shore on a surfboard was so picturesque I couldn't
stifle a smile. Paul knew what I was thinking, and he laughed
too.

"Surfing keeps me in touch with the peacefulness out here
at the ocean, and I love it. I used to run a lot, but I hurt my

knee, had surgery, and can't run much anymore."

I wondered why some physical problems could be healed and others weren't responsive to treatment. Here was a powerful healer who couldn't help his own knees. Strange.

I would have loved to explore that subject, but Paul had to leave for his appointment. I had a long, leisurely walk, undisturbed by the few people running or strolling. We seemed to share a common bond, we ocean-lovers who were willing to give up sleep to be out to greet the morning sea in the gentle early light. It set the tone for a peaceful, quiet day.

When I got back to the house, Joyce was up and bustling about the kitchen, dressed in a turquoise terry robe exactly like one I had at home. Once again I found myself looking hard for similarities, wondering why I needed them.

We sat down at the kitchen table to talk for a while before I left. We spoke of our lives, reluctant to part, but Joyce had a lot to do; she and Paul were leaving on a business trip to New York the next day.

Contact

When I drove home through the flower-starred hills, I felt blessed to have been with loving people who were actually living new-age philosophy.

I was in a euphoric mood, supremely confident of my ability to enjoy life and find new, exciting dimensions to it. I felt that the car drove *me* home; the wheels found no bump on the road, the sunlight sparkled on the ocean, roadside roofs, cars. I drove for an hour, then detoured to Laguna for lunch. When I arrived home in the early afternoon, I apologized to Moose for her empty food bowl the night before.

After I fed her and put away my things, I got out my book and wrote: I'm home now, feeling serene and elated, and most content with my life. Was Paul Brenner correct in saying that I do not need more teachers?

He is indeed.

Why? Part of me still feels lacking in the ability to focus my energy.

It is done for you. It is now well done for you. Do not doubt, for FAILURE IS DOUBT DRESSED IN REAL

*CLOTHES. There is in you a center of utmost calm
.....there is a new force here that will refresh you
now. It is a lack of conflict. Conflict stirs the waters
and thirsts the soul.*

The calmness lasted only a short time.

Two nights later I went to bed, cuddled briefly with Larry
and fell asleep immediately. Awakened by a full bladder a few
hours later, I stumbled out of bed and into the bathroom.
When I got back to bed I couldn't fall asleep. I didn't fight the
wakefulness, but contented myself with warm and loving
thoughts of the Brenners, who now must be in New York. I
wondered languidly if they felt as warm toward me as I did
toward them, and decided they did. Nice to feel good about
myself, I thought, and turned over on my side to get in my
favorite sleeping position.

Suddenly my reverie was interrupted by strong, precise
images: I was once again in the tranquil meditation room by
the Brenner's pool. I was in a happy, gay mood. Paul turned
to me and I began to write. I realized with a shock that the
cramped, tiny word coming out on paper was frightening,
terrifying in the ramifications I knew underlay the letters:

chemicals

I knew positively that I'd gotten in touch with someone
who was deeply into drugs. The imagery continued, and I saw
myself turning away from Paul to hide the panic in me. I felt
myself in a dense, black, dangerous hole. I began to take on
the frantic helplessness of someone I didn't know, but who
seemed a part of Paul. I watched myself as in a movie while
the drama continued: I got to my feet, walked slowly to the
sliding door, opened it, and walked into the pool with my
clothes and shoes on. I stood in the shallow end of the Brenner's pool and put my face into the water so that I couldn't
breathe. Then, gasping and choking, I looked up and said,
"Help me! Oh, help me! I'm drowning!"

I was a strong, secure swimmer—why would I have an
image of myself in such a bizarre dramatization of drowning?
The whole scene was as real as the bed I was in. It began

repeating, over and over, like a bad meal that refused to be digested: the same word written, the same emotions of fear, terror, drowning.

I got up again and went to the kitchen for a drink of water, then walked around the den to break the mood and disconnect the imagery. I found Moose in Denise's room, petted her, rearranged the covers on Denny and returned to bed to confront the same powerful imagery as before. It seemed most peculiar that it never altered an iota: conversations, dreams, fantasies, automatic writing all grew, changed, expanded. Not this. It was brilliantly delineated and crisp; I saw every thread of carpet in the meditation room, each drop of water in the pool as it dripped from me.

Now I was not only wide awake, but thoroughly upset. My rational mind intruded and said: stay out of this mess! Stay out! But still the visualization continued, marching through my mind like a stuck record.

At last, I rolled over and woke Larry. "Turn over, honey," he said. "I'll cuddle you." But his warm body was not enough to soothe me to sleep.

I had the idea that I could test or put to rest the whole dilemma by calling on my guide, Paul, in my thoughts. I'd never done that before; I only asked for help when I wrote. But now I voiced the words: please help. If this vision is accurate, help me reach the Brenners—wherever they are in New York. At least make me know if this is true or false. Make me know it—please!

I felt a strange pulsation around my heart that moved to my throat. It was throbbing, frightening because it was unknown—a potent force unlike anything I'd ever experienced. Suddenly my legs started vibrating, cramping and contracting. I'd had severe leg cramps in my life, and this was not at all similar; there was no pain. The contractions moved in rhythmic pulsations up each leg from my feet and I was rocked by the strong currents that were charging through my body. I threw my pillow to the floor and lay down next to the bed where I had meditated for so many years. I wanted desperately to psychically reach Paul, to warn him of drug and drowning danger to someone close to him.

The vibrating, energized waves continued but the imagery changed suddenly. I saw Paul in the country on a porch looking at some curved shape in a field just beyond him. I was sure the setting was wrong; New York City meant tall, greyed skyscrapers and asphalt streets.

The energy, rather than diminishing, became stronger. I felt attacked, terrorized and utterly alone on the floor, and moved back to bed. The clock showed it was 4 a.m.

Exhausted, drained physically and mentally, I began to cry. Larry woke up and held me close while I poured out the whole story. "I wish you'd never gotten involved with all this psychic shit," he said. "Promise me you'll stop all this nonsense from now on."

I couldn't promise, and I felt abandoned by him when I desperately needed help. Frightened as I was, I didn't believe I had summoned the energy. I felt like a television set that was screening a drama; I didn't know how to turn it off, but surely I wasn't responsible for turning the channel to something so relentless, so lingering. No psychic phenomenon had ever lasted this long or had this much power behind it.

I fell asleep toward dawn, utterly depleted.

I half-expected a call from the Brenners the next day, and I chided myself for foolishly thinking I'd made a connection, yet half-hoping I had. I didn't hear from them; now I questioned whether I should say anything when they returned. I could be butting into a family situation that didn't exist, that might never take place. How could I couch what I'd felt in words that would disguise the worry and urgency I felt that someone, possibly their son—whom I'd never met—was in danger? I felt trapped and upset, unsure of myself. I didn't doubt I'd had the experience, but I was concerned about being subjected to a psychic battering that might bring a problem into a relationship I hoped would be a smooth one. Larry wanted me to drop the whole thing, but I couldn't. It festered for days.

Certain the Brenners must be home from New York, I called on the pretext of ordering more copies of his book, *Health is a Question of Balance.* No sooner had I given the order than I blurted out the whole episode to Paul.

"What night was the dream?" he asked.

"Well, it would have been your second night in New York."

"Bobbie, the night you had the dream we were staying at my sister's house on Long Island. It's exactly as you described it: she has a large home and a porch overlooking extensive grounds with a curving stream. I often get up early, go out on the porch and look out at the view. In fact, I probably was out there at the exact time all the energy was going through you. What you also couldn't have known was that my sister had a son I loved deeply. My nephew was a wonderful kid—bright, athletic and talented; he got into trouble with drugs when he was at college. He'd been on the swimming team, but when the drugs took over, he couldn't do anything. He really wanted to straighten himself out, and everyone else tried to help, but he just couldn't seem to make it. Then he decided to go to one of his favorite spots, Puerta Vallarta, to see if he could let go of his demons in a quiet place away from everyone and come home OK. One day this champion swimmer went down to the ocean for a swim and drowned. It happened nine years ago, Bobbie. I haven't been back to New York in years, but when I went to my sister's, I couldn't help but be sad all over again at the loss of such a beautiful life. You picked up all of that."

I was utterly overcome with a sense of deliverance, that what I'd seen was the past and not a warning of a future death. I hung up, buried my head in my arms, and said a quiet prayer of thanks—and relief.

Issues

My reaction to the drowning episode raised many issues.

It took me days to even begin to *want* to sort it out, for the emotional intensity stayed with me and I was drained of energy, left with a lingering list of unanswered questions. When I felt more centered and able to think clearly, I attempted to assess what had happened.

I never thought I was a medium. A reference book I had checked said mediums got information through trance states; I didn't do that. Also, if I had any choice in the matter, I didn't *want* to be a medium. The question of choice was a central issue in many ways: I wanted to be involved with parapsychology, but I didn't look forward to receiving any more news of illness or death. Did I even HAVE a choice?

The simplest explanation was that, after all this time, I still wasn't protecting myself enough. I was often careless and no longer said any invocation to be protected by the Light when I was home and just writing for myself; it was like strapping oneself in a safety belt to drive to the corner; I just didn't take the time. When I sat down to type away in the security of my own home I *felt* protected, whether or not I really was;

if I did any psychic work with strangers, I tended to be a little more cautious.

Every teacher I had worked with in the past few years warned students that there were both positive and negative forces in the universe, and to be open, to be sensitive, if one was not aware, was to court problems. To be able to 'tune in' to others, to receive psychic input, required defenses; imaging the Light as a protective, surrounding force, invoking the aid and help of the benevolent spirits and guides. Strangely, I still felt peculiar asking for help I could neither see nor feel; I was perfectly comfortable when Paul wrote through me, but still felt odd when I asked for protection. I'd better change and start to request all the help I could get.

But the telepathy with Paul Brenner had been spontaneous, not invoked. I'd had no warning that I might even be getting into any extra-sensory perception. The distance gap had been over 3,000 miles, although I knew time and space meant nothing in the transmission of such energy. But something *was* changing, and I needed to make up my mind as to what was healthiest for me... and see if it worked.

Although I usually wrote in a positive, cheerful vein, it was simple for me to pick up the emotional resonation of illness, trauma, and death, physically as well as emotionally; a point on my chestbone reverberated to pain in others. How long before I began to manifest the symptoms, then the disease? It was no more far-fetched than precognition, or the laying-on of hands to heal. The price was too high to pay.

It was easy to say I didn't want any more of all that, but the experiences had also provided a human connection that made me feel more empathy for others than I'd ever believed possible. The caring about others, the touching of their lives, had opened up MY life more than it had depressed me, and the automatic writing had forged a link that left me with a deep sense of communion and love.

If I determined not to be a receiver of any negativity, would I lose ALL connections to the psychic world I loved to explore?

This was an issue I had been evading, although I'd had plenty of warning in the pattern of psychic experiences in the past year. It seemed I was a 'sensitive,' and as such, incidents

were apt to occur whether I wanted them or not. As long as
they had been light and rather fun, such as the 'apples' incident from Dr. Moss' class, I was delighted with the paranormal powers; when they got heavy and depressing, as with
Paul Brenner's nephew, I wanted to back off. But many teachers, such as Ram Dass—in his book, *Grist for the Mill*—had
mentioned that ALL powers (called *siddhis* by the Hindus),
are in themselves traps because they tend to get the individual stuck in his ego, effectively separating him (or her)
from others.

I thought: when in doubt, ask Paul—the ethereal Paul. My
hand wrote:

> *It be the time to see life as a whole and not as small
> parts. By perceiving wholeness, the self aligns its
> energies to that of a different density, and in that
> space can attune to vibrations which are radiant and
> healing. If you persist in being attached to the events
> that take place, then you will miss the Path, which
> is to become whole through being loving, by attuning
> to one-ness, whole-ness.*

> *Then the self crosses a bridge to another place, which
> is neither demanding nor controlling. An event be-
> comes just that—no more and no less. The powers
> you have sensed are present in all, and are not unusual.*

> *To stay trapped in their availability is to deny pro-
> gress—progress of the self towards a higher order,
> one that needs no words nor events to know the Crea-
> tor, the Source. Events are to make you rethink in
> larger terms, to escape the smallness of rigid percep-
> tion, to break through into a world in which it is
> only necessary TO BE. If you do not be judging the
> experience with the drowned boy, then it be nothing
> more than a sign you be connecting to others. Let go
> of the need to explain. There is great peace in this.*

> *Man has splintered his experiences by the assumption
> that others be wrong and he be right.*

Asilomar

The week between Christmas and New Years was a 'dead' one as far as Larry's business was concerned, and we took the opportunity to go to a special five-day celebration with Brugh Joy and a few hundred other people. I was thrilled that Larry was so willing to attend, and hopeful that we'd have decent weather. The conference site, Asilomar, was on the ocean in the beautiful Carmel-Monterey area, noted for its rugged beauty as well as thick, cold fogs and chilling winter rain storms.

The accommodations were in buildings scattered around the grounds, rather like dormitories on a college campus. Ours was a contemporary design, set along a pathway that was the equivalent of several blocks from the meeting hall. Most of the buildings were old and rustic, but all had cozy 'living rooms' on each floor, with plenty of wood provided for the fireplaces.

I discovered many people I knew as we registered, and thought happily that the time would be a renewal of friend-ships as well as of spirit.

We were disappointed when we heard that the Brenners had to cancel. Paul had been scheduled to lead a small group; Brugh had divided us into sections of about fifteen people and these units met twice a day in the comfortable living rooms with rotating teachers. Larry and I were in different groups.

Brugh, who loved to do things with style, had been thoughtful enough to provide a thick carpet for the huge, hard-floored, drafty hall in which we met morning and evening. Like the Sky Hi sessions, we listened to music lying down. The format was similar to that at the ranch, with afternoons free. Music and dance were scheduled in the main hall for those who wished to attend; some preferred to read, rest, or walk; Larry found a friend who'd also brought golf clubs and they played one of the area's outstanding courses every day.

It was idyllic in every respect: the weather was spectacularly clear and crisp; the ocean, a few hundred yards beyond us, was deep blues and greens, the waves wreathed in whitecaps that spent themselves upon a broad beach ideal for walking or jogging. One end of the curved sand beach ended in massive spilled boulders, as though a giant hand had carelessly thrown them like grey dice. We sat on high dunes and watched the whales traveling south, their spouts and occasional up-thrust tails giving their positions away.

Shy, curious deer wandered through the conference grounds, maintaining an aloof distance with serene dignity and quiet grace. The crisp days and cold nights left a white frost coating on plants and trees that glittered and faded in the morning sunlight as the animal tracks melted into the ground.

Brugh and his co-leader, David Spangler, had a full program of outstanding speakers, as well as musicians who performed at every meeting. Elisabeth Kübler-Ross was the special guest, and she fascinated Larry as she had me when I had heard her speak at my first holistic conference. The woman glowed with intensity and sincerity; I watched her as she answered questions near the refreshment tables during the break, and I was captivated by her directness—she never took her eyes from the questioner, and never seemed to want to get away or evade an issue. I managed a brief moment to thank her for helping me deal with my mother's illness, for I'd read her books about death and dying and had found them great comforts.

Music filtered through the tall pines and into our hearts, marking the morning 'get-up' call each day, and ending with an evening serenade.

My favorite musician was Larkin, a sensitive flutist; I asked to shoot pictures of him, and late one afternoon, I followed him to the beach as he played and walked—a new-age, bearded Pied Piper. Just before sunset, he climbed the rocks to play as the sun reddened, purpled, and dipped to the horizon. I shot roll after roll, sure I had something special. Two years later, his album, O'Cean, came out with one of my shots on the cover: his silhouette with flute against the sea and the sunset.

The day before New Year's Eve, Brugh announced that we would have twenty-four hours of silence. Fasting was optional, and juices would be provided for those who wished. I didn't think I wanted to fast, but the long silence was an unknown that sounded interesting.

With no option but to be quiet or break the common consent, the day became a shared experience of peace and blissful quiet punctuated only by the far-off sound of seals barking brought in on the breeze. I found a shift in consciousness accelerated by the stillness; without the need or opportunity to make social talk, with no self-demands for food or busyness, the day unrolled in golden splendor and heightened awareness. I knew what Larry wanted to do as he knew of me: we found ourselves rising together to take a walk, get juice, and take a book to the dunes to read. There was no *need* to speak, for we found our tempo to be as one; we wandered through the day holding hands, or drawing our initials on the sand with a pointed stick. It was magical, like some romantic dream that had actually come true; our hearts spoke without words.

Brugh provided a magnificent New Year's ceremony, complete with music, candles, and blessings for the coming year. He had a sense of pace and appropriateness for his remarks, and we sent energy to the planet, to all people, and basked in it ourselves. He had made no attempt, other than the silent period, to coerce us into anything other than enjoying the

conference peace. It was remarkable how well he'd accomplished his intent.

We stayed a day later than most, visited our daughter, Linda, in Santa Cruz, and then packed up to drive back to Los Angeles. I drove first as Larry slept, and noted storm clouds massing on the horizon. There was not a breath of air stirring the trees, and I thought we'd probably make it home before the weather turned nasty. I couldn't decide between taking the coast route—the more scenic trip—or the quicker, inland road, so I turned on the radio, realizing as I did so that it was set for Los Angeles stations and not for northern ones. At the very instant I turned on the radio, a man's voice said clearly, as though he'd heard my question, "All cars and campers stay off the ridge route. High winds of 80 mph forecast, with extreme danger to all vehicles."

"Thank you," I said to the radio, and took the coastal highway.

Faces

'*Synchronicity*' is a word I learned in metaphysical study; it describes seemingly random events not as coincidences, but connected in a meaningful way, although we may not always perceive the interrelatedness. I had a marvelous example that supported my new-found belief in the synchronicity of events.

On Friday, May 18, Larry and I arrived home from a long trip. Among many accumulated phone calls, I found an exciting message that *Los Angeles Magazine* had a writing assignment for me.

When I called the magazine, they gave me the name of a well-known plastic surgeon in Beverly Hills whom I was to interview. He was known for a process called a 'face peel.' It sounded like a dream assignment incorporating everything I loved to do: research, interview and photography, all on an interesting subject. I made an appointment to meet the doctor the following Monday.

Prompt as usual, I entered his immaculately neat reception area, introduced myself to the pleasant secretary, and was immediately ushered in to meet Dr. S. I set up my tape recorder in his cluttered office and, after the amenities, asked some simple questions about his work.

"What IS a chemical face peel?" I began.

He said, "It's a chemical—a caustic one—that causes the skin to burn, scab, and repair itself with new, perfect skin. No surgery is involved."

I nodded, taking notes.

"*Mine* is the best," he added proudly.

"How is your process different from or better than anyone else's?" I asked. He began to defend himself in long, rambling statements, as if I had attacked him.

"I'm the best," he said again, but quickly averted his eyes. "I have a magic formula and a secret way of taping the face after it's done that makes it as good as a surgical face lift."

"Where did you study and train? I'd like to hear about your background and your work." He insisted I get up and look at the credentials hanging on a wall. As I made notes, he began defending himself again. It made me wonder if the credentials were legitimate. I was reminded of Richard Nixon saying, "I am not a crook." The doctor even bore a faint resemblance to Nixon: dark, deep-set eyes, shadowed jowls, and a certain intensity that was making me feel uncomfortable.

"Here. Look at these magazines." He shoved the National Enquirer and a movie magazine at me. As I scanned the articles, which implied he had done everyone from Sophia to Liz without actually stating so, he kept talking in strange, tangential statements. "Have lunch with me at the Brown Derby, and I'll really give you some names, plus a lot of juicy anecdotes. I'll give you everything you need," he said, and I was not unaware of the double entendre and the half-smile on his face. I was getting very nervous and tried to stay calm.

"How about some pictures of you?" I asked.

"Of course," he said, and erupted into a scream at an unseen associate through the half-open door. "Do my hair! NOW!"

A very pretty woman scurried in and began styling and spraying his hair as I set up my camera and tripod and looked for the best shots.

The woman disappeared and Dr. S. assumed a dramatic attitude, swiveling his desk chair and alternately smiling and scowling, showing me various poses. He looked into space with a brooding stare and seemed disoriented, as though he was over-acting a part in a silent film. It was utterly absurd.

The photographs would have been terrible; the mess on his desk was impossible to avoid and his pose was ridiculous. Normally, I would have asked to remove or stack the papers and give directions for the pose I wanted, but everything in me was rebelling.

He noticed my hestitation. "I want my antiques to show."

I was damply nervous, needing to feel in control but not knowing what to do or say. I stalled for time. "I'd rather come back, interview you some more, and bring additional lighting equipment. That will give you a chance to arrange the office the way you wish."

He wanted me to shoot the photographs but was unsure how far to push me.

I tried to lighten the tension between us. "Do you know of an excellent restaurant in this area? It's my husband's birthday today, and I want to take him out for a special lunch."

He yelled at an invisible staffmember: "Get a reservation for two at the Bistro! *Mention my name.*"

I heard no response to this order, and neither, apparently, did he, for he screamed louder, rage barely under control: "Do it NOW!"

I said lamely, "Oh, don't bother. I'm not even sure my husband can make it."

"Call him! Call him *right now. I* am paying for your lunch. I wish the limousine were here to take you." He spoke hurriedly, through thin lips, and pushed the phone at me.

I panicked, realizing I was being bribed as well as overpowered, knowing I was out of my league in dealing with the doctor. I dialed Larry's office. At my insistence his secretary cut in on him as he was on a long distance call.

"What's up? I'm on an important call. I'll phone you back."

"I'm sorry you can't make lunch. I'll stop by in half an hour or so, and see if we can have something brought to your office if you're too busy to go out. And say 'hello' to Jim for me."

Larry knew me well enough to wonder what was making me lie so blatantly. He hadn't cancelled the lunch and he wasn't speaking to Jim. "Are you OK?" he asked.

"I'll see you in a little while. Bye, honey." I wondered if I sounded as nervous as I was; I felt like a ball of yarn unraveling. I left the doctor with his promise that he'd call me as soon as he had a patient who would allow me to photograph the face peel procedure, and at that time we'd finish the interview and shoot portraits as well as shots of him at work.

When Larry and I went to lunch I couldn't stop trembling. I was physically terrified of something unknown, as well as feeling an enormous aversion to Dr. S. I felt contaminated, and the words, *"he is evil,"* kept running through my mind. I'd never had such an immediate, negative reaction to anyone. He'd directed his anger at others, yet I felt as though I'd been beaten by a crazy man. I told Larry the whole story of my morning, and even his wonderful sense of humor didn't appreciably lighten my mood.

The phone rang at eight the next morning. Larry answered; he was shockingly rude. "Doctor, I do not allow my wife to take personal calls before 9 a.m." He hung up abruptly, and when I asked the reason for his outrageous behavior, he laughingly said, "Well, you did mention you didn't like him."

"But it's my assignment," I wailed. "You have no right to interfere like that!"

"Dump him," he smiled, and hugged me.

I called the doctor after Larry left for work. "Who the hell answers the phone like that?" he asked, and I found myself apologizing for my husband's roughness. "Well, I have good news, after all," he continued pleasantly. "I have a patient coming in for eyelid surgery and a face peel at noon today, and she's given her permission to have you photograph her. She'll sign the model release."

I was excited. Maybe yesterday had been a bad day all around. It was certainly going to be an interesting story; perhaps I'd get more space than the small article they'd assigned. I wondered how well I'd stand the sight of blood. I couldn't wait to get my camera and lighting equipment loaded in the car.

I was kept waiting in the reception room, told the surgery had started late. When I was ushered into the small operating room, the patient was out cold on the table and an intravenous solution was going into her arm. Dr. S. lowered his surgical mask and smiled benignly at me.

"Wait in the doorway," he said. "I can't let you get any closer, since you're not sterilized. Can you shoot from there? I want you to have FUN. We have some fresh coffee in the little room over there, so go get yourself a cup and then come back and you can start shooting."

I did as I was told, elated over the way the session was beginning. While the photographic angle from the doorway was not ideal, I'd brought my zoom lens and it would still be very workable. I had two cameras and three lenses with me, and with the second camera and close-up lens I shot pictures of the patient's 'before' photos pinned to the wall near me.

Two other white-gowned people were attending the patient, who now had her lower eyelids held out by forceps (or something metal), while the doctor worked over her. There was not much blood and she was obviously deeply sedated, for she never moved a muscle. My concentration was bothered by the noise level; the three of them were talking, rock music was blaring in the room, and pop songs were wafting in from the reception area.

The doctor finished stitching under both eyes and came over to me, casually brushing my breast with his elbow. He smiled. I smiled weakly. I hate him, I thought; looking at this surgery doesn't make me sick—he does. And he's even *more* repulsive when he's smiling.

There was a short break before the doctor's assistant began the face peel. I realized I'd met her the day before—she had styled his hair. I was told she wasn't allowed to do the surgery because she wasn't a doctor, but was permitted to do the peel by herself since it didn't involve any surgery.

She began by taking a sable brush, dipping it in a chemical and gently painting the patient's forehead. Nothing happened that I could see, yet we were all standing around waiting. Dr. S. explained that the skin is an organ of the body and must not absorb the potent chemical too quickly. No blisters formed, no change took place. I was sure nothing dramatic would show in the pictures: it looked as though the unconscious subject was being painted with invisible ink. Each area of the face was done slowly, finished by feather strokes along the jawline.

"At this point, the skin is like wet concrete," Dr. S. said. "I have a secret technique of wrapping so that she'll look like she's had plastic surgery to lift her face, instead of a nonsurgical peel. I can't let you shoot the beginning of it—trade secrets, you know—so go have another cup of coffee and I'll call you when we're ready for you to shoot again. Are you having FUN?"

I was both repelled and fascinated, and welcomed a moment to myself.

When they called me back I began shooting the cocoon of gauze being wound about the head. She looked like a creature from outer space: small slits were left for her eyes, nostrils, and mouth; her head was a basket-sized balloon of white cotton. She began to stir and make small sounds. I promised myself I would never, ever have this done to me.

The doctor again brushed my breast as he strode out. "Come to my office, and we can continue the interview and you can shoot the portraits of me. While I'm cleaning up, you might want to talk to one of my patients who is in for her one-year checkup."

I was ushered into a small cubicle and introduced to an attractive woman in her 30s with translucent skin that looked as clear and porcelain as a china cup.

"I came in originally for a nose job, but decided to have a face peel too. My skin was really blemished, especially around my neck." She showed me her 'before' picture. She looked like a new woman compared to the pitted, hook-nosed creature in the photo.

Maybe I'm being silly to distrust Dr. S., I thought; after all, his personality shouldn't be important if his results are this impressive.

But his character WAS important to me, as I realized ten

minutes later back in his office. He was more relaxed than
yesterday, but still he screamed orders to others in a demeaning way.

"How about having a drink with me at the Brown Derby
this weekend?" he asked. "I'm a total tyrant in the office—
a real S.O.B.—but I'm a LOT of fun outside." My stomach
turned and growled loudly as I set up my tape recorder.

"Can I print that you admit you're a tyrant?" I asked, seeing
a sudden glimmer of a way to write the article and still tell
the truth about him.

"Sure. I don't give a shit. I don't drink or carouse during
the week. I give my best to my patients, and the worst to my
help." He paused, contemplative. "Yes, an S.O.B. is one of
the nicer things I've been called." He seemed proud of his
tough reputation, and the slight thaw I'd felt for him after
meeting his patient hardened as he continued to talk in circles, bragging about his celebrity patients and dangling their
unspoken names in front of me like a carrot in front of a horse.
It was a boastful, rambling monologue that needed no questions from me. I shot a few uninspired portraits to back up
the article and pacify him, said my goodbyes, gathered my
equipment and staggered to my car. I was glad I wouldn't
have to see any of them for another week, at which time I'd
photograph his patient in a recuperative stage of the face
peel. She did not seem human to me at all—just a 'thing;' I
wanted to get to know her as a woman who had chosen this
alteration of herself.

As I rewound my film, I noticed a telltale lack of tension
in the spool, and I leaned against the fender, unwilling to see
what must be the truth. Should I find out now or later?

Now.

When I opened the back of the Nikon that I'd used to photograph the surgery, I gasped in horror. I'd forgotten to load it
with film! The dumbest mistake of them all! I'd never done
that before, and there was no going back on this job. I felt
sick to my stomach for my stupidity—at all the feelings this
job had brought on. I didn't have the guts to admit to the
doctor that I'd made the most amateurish goof of my life.
I was sure he'd attack me verbally, if not physically. What had
been wrong with me?

In addition to everything else, I was very late for an important engagement; we had dinner plans with the president and
his wife of Larry's most important company. At least I really
enjoyed the Olsens. I just hated me. I resolved to get out of
photography forever. What could I tell the magazine? On the
other hand, how would they know what other pictures I'd
shot, if the two rolls with my close-up lens were good? I drove
home through rush hour traffic, delivered the two rolls of
exposed film, and got ready for dinner, determined to be light
and pleasant.

My disgust with myself and aversion to the doctor continued after a delightful dinner and a futile attempt to fall
asleep. I couldn't make myself get up and start typing. I knew
I'd be blitzed when the alarm went off at 6:30 a.m. and I'd had
only a couple of hours of sleep.

I was at the typewriter by eight, describing Dr. S. as running
his office with all the timidity of General Patton under attack.
After all, it WAS war—war on aging. I would not make the
doctor nice; I would tell the truth.

When I told the tale and read the brief rough draft to my
writing friends the next day, they thought my story had good
possibilities. But one of the women mentioned something
that had haunted me all week. "Where is your responsibility
to your intuition, Bobbie?" she asked. "You know you're
sensitive, you know you're psychic."

Where indeed was the ethical, moral me who trusted herself
enough to know there was something very wrong with the
doctor? The one good job and satisfied patient I'd seen was
not enough. I'd have to do more research about him, and go
to a dispassionate source.

I asked a friend for the name of the plastic surgeon who'd
done such a good job on her, and made an appointment to
see the surgeon the following day. I postponed writing any
more until I'd heard his opinions.

On Friday, I was kept waiting in Doctor W's office for an
hour and a half until he had seen all his patients. That was
only fair, and it gave me an excellent opportunity to study
those in his waiting room and to scan the book he'd written
about surgical and non-surgical cosmetic rejuvenation.

At last the receptionist ushered me in to meet Dr. W. He wore a tight nylon sport shirt and slim pants that showed off his lean body. The pointed boots were very trendy.

I decided to level with him. "I was told to interview Dr. S. for *Los Angeles Magazine*," I began, "But I'm here because you're a top surgeon who might be able to give me a professional slant—you see, I'm terribly upset about Dr. S. A funny feeling tells me that something is very wrong, but I don't know what it is. I'd really appreciate your help."

He didn't pause at all to consider his words, which exploded like TNT in my ears: "Dr. S. is the scum of the earth. He's the slimiest human being I've ever met, and I've worked with him. He'd tell you anything to get publicity! *Why* the man is allowed to practice, I'll never know. He's a liar, he's crazy and he's dangerous!"

I couldn't believe one doctor would say such damning things about another. I hadn't even had time to plug in my cassette recorder. I did so now, and he continued his blast as I mentioned some of the claims Dr. S. had bragged about.

"What about his statement that his face peel is unique— a magic chemical formula?"

"Bullshit," he growled. "All the stuff is similar...he just buys his chemicals at a different store. And if he *did* have that magic formula he claims, I think less of him for not sharing what could benefit so many people. As for his 'unique taping' process, if you have loose, hanging skin, a peel and taping won't fix it—the excess skin has to go somewhere; it has to be surgically cut away. The man is a liar! A congenital liar! Besides which, he charges outrageous prices."

I left after a twenty-minute conversation in which everything Dr. S. had told me was refuted in no uncertain terms. I liked Dr. W., and certainly appreciated his time, but as I drove home in the bumper-to-bumper traffic I was totally confused. If I believed Dr. S. did good—not miraculous—work in chemical peels, then I had to report that. After all, it was my assignment. If I exposed him as an overpriced fraud, as Dr. W. had suggested, then I could be open to a lawsuit, and, I was sure—personal retaliation. I believed there was nothing he would stop at—for either fame or revenge—and I couldn't put both sides in the article; this was not to be an exposé.

I didn't have the nerve to write one even if the magazine would approve that slant.

I arrived home exhausted. When Larry got in shortly afterwards, we sat down with our wine to talk about the latest scene in this comic opera. I needed to calm down. Friends soon would be joining us for dinner and bridge.

The doorbell rang and I jumped up to answer it, thinking the Morans had come early. There stood a total stranger, waiting expectantly to be invited in. He introduced himself, extended his hand to shake mine, and said, "Hi. I'm Tom Connors. I'm here for your class. I hope I'm not too early."

"Class? What class?"

Larry came up to find out what was happening. Suddenly, I remembered. "Oh—my friend was teaching a writing workshop here. We were just lending our home. But she cancelled it because she didn't get enough people to sign up; she told me last night she had reached everyone but one man, and he'd changed jobs and phone."

"I'm the one. It was a mix-up all around. I'll be going— sorry I disturbed you."

Larry said, "Too bad you made the trip in vain. Care to come in and have a glass of wine with us?"

Tom accepted, and we sat down in the den, chatting about the current gas shortage, the class he hoped would be rescheduled, and other mundane events. He appeared to be a pleasant, rather shy man; I was only half listening, my mind still on the interview with Dr. W. It would have taken an earthquake to make me pay full attention to anything other than my inner dialogue.

Not usually curious about what others did for a living, I surprised myself by asking, "What do you do when you're not taking writing workshops?"

Tom smiled and said, "I'm an investigator for the State of California. I work on medical frauds."

It didn't dawn on me that it was miraculous for him to show up at my door just when I needed some help to determine the fate of the story.

"If you've been watching Connie Chung on the 6 o'clock news, she's been exposing some abortion clinics—an investigation I worked on."

The doorbell rang. Our friends came in, introductions were made all around, and Tom said, "I don't want to interrupt your plans."

"You're not." I refilled his glass. "I'm very interested in what you just said. I'm in the middle of writing an article about a doctor who does non-surgical face peels."

"What?" He put his drink down carefully, sat very erect, and said precisely and firmly, "Watch out. You just don't know what you're getting into."

I told the events of the past week, including the interview two hours before with Dr. W. "Well, HE'S reputable, I'll say that for him, but I am warning you in the strongest way I know how: *Stay away from the story, and especially from Dr. S.!*"

He spoke so urgently, in such a worried tone. "May I tape what you have to say?"

"No. Oh, no. But I'll give you a name in Sacramento to call if you want more information. You'll get my boss; please promise me you won't mention how you got his number. I'm afraid you'll have to take my word you're on very dangerous ground. I can't say it strongly enough! And I really must leave. Thank you for your hospitality."

After he'd gone, we four sat in stunned disbelief, speechless as we realized the odds against this man coming to my door at the precise moment I needed help. The ramifications went beyond the publishing of a story. Synchronicity explained it all, in my belief system, and I gave silent thanks for having my prayers answered so directly. A tiny part of me still wanted to be published by the magazine, but the wiser part knew I had to stay out. I just didn't know how much to tell them.

Saturday morning, after a restless night, I looked at our date book to see what we were doing that evening. The week had been so tumultuous I couldn't recall making social plans. A name scribbled in for tonight made me smile—long-ago plans with friends we saw only a few times a year. He was a surgeon who had studied law and was now active in malpractice cases.

After dinner and my long-winded story, Dudley got right to his opinion. "Do you need the money?"

"I've already mentally spent it. But I really want to establish myself as someone who can do it all: write, shoot pictures, do research; money isn't really the issue—my ethics and career are."

"You'll be giving this madman exactly what he wants—free publicity. It wouldn't even matter if it's a negative opinion; the magazine has enormous influence. If there should be a lawsuit against him and the patient had found him because she just remembered seeing his name in your article, you could be called to testify if it came to trial. What on earth do you need all this for? Stay away!"

I had the home phone number of the assigning editor and saw her on Sunday to resign from the story. What would have been a feast for an exposé writer was something I couldn't handle. The warnings had been only too clear. If I lacked courage, well...perhaps it was not my time to be brave.

Party

Larry and I were late arriving at the dinner party. We knew no one but the host and hostess, who were busy circulating among the two dozen guests. Conversation bubbling from the fashionably dressed, slightly intoxicated people was predictably superficial and very dull—dull at least for me, for I had little interest in country clubs, maid problems, and the current divorces and remarriages of strangers.

I wished we'd stayed at home...I felt irritable and anti-social. As I drank my wine, I looked around the garden and critically, unkindly, saw us all as middle-aged, middle-class people having a mindless evening. I looked as though I belonged here, and I resented that most.

At last the hostess urged us inside to dinner, where we separated to two tables, beautifully garnished with perfectly coordinated linens, china and silver. A rich dinner was served by solicitous waiters. Conversation was sporadic as everyone ate; we were all much too well-bred to talk with our mouths full. Surreptitiously I tried to loosen my silk slacks.

A waiter began to fill the delicately patterned cups with coffee, and during the discreet quiet as we awaited our turn a greying man across the table asked with no great interest but with an obvious attempt to fill a void, "Bobbie, what do *you* do?"

"Well," I answered, "I'm a photographer, a writer and... a healer." I heard myself add the last word and was surprised I'd said it. My answer, spoken quietly, was easily heard in the room, and I was at once the center of attention, the focus of stares.

Silence. Even the waiter paused and looked startled.

Larry smiled and put his arm around my shoulders. He told everyone of my 'miracle' healing of his bursitis, no longer a milestone to me but intriguing, apparently, to the others.

I got ready for the sarcastic questions I knew would come. I became aware that the woman to my right, who had barely spoken all night, had a severe headache. She hadn't said so, but I felt it in a sudden throb of awareness.

"How's your headache?" I asked, turning to her and smiling.

A frightened, hesitant pause. "How do you know I have one?"

She didn't wait for my answer and continued in a low voice, "I've had constant, severe headaches for several months. I'm never free of pain. The medications the doctors have prescribed give me nausea and high blood pressure. I just don't know what to do anymore. All the tests were negative for brain tumors."

There was a murmur of sympathy for her; under it I felt hostility coming toward me from somewhere on my left, and I looked up to see a large man staring at me intently. His arms were crossed, his lips pursed. "My wife has been to the best doctors. No one can help Sandy."

"I may be able to help you get rid of the pain, at least temporarily," I said to her.

"What are you going to do?" Sandy asked quietly, apprehensively.

We both seemed to be a bit sorry we were enmeshed in the discussion. She obviously felt she'd aired too much of her private troubles in front of strangers. I felt like a woman about to make a fool of herself.

"Go ahead. Heal her. I want to see *that*," someone said in a high laugh that ended in a giggle.

I eased myself off the patterned velvet chair and stood behind Sandy.

"May I touch you?" I asked.

"Yes." She was breathing unevenly, and I felt her shrinking beneath me as her husband stood up to make sure I wasn't going to harm his wife.

I continued, "I won't crack your neck or manipulate your body in any way. Most of the time my hands won't be on you at all. Just listen to the sound of my voice with your eyes closed. I'll let you know when we're through. OK?"

She nodded timidly, like a child about to be punished by a stern teacher in front of the class. Her husband checked in again and said, "Sandy, are you willing to do this?"

"Yes. I'll try anything."

I stood behind her, resting my hands very lightly on her shoulders and feeling my energies beginning to move toward an unseen but focused center in me. I asked inaudibly that I be a healing channel of energy for the body before me, that I be protected from any negative or harmful energy in the room.

"Sandy, please put your feet flat on the floor and rest your hands in your lap. Begin breathing slowly, exhaling through your mouth. Now—and this is the most important part—give yourself permission to let go of the pain. Say that to yourself, over and over, as your body begins to relax and you follow the sound of my voice and the warmth of my hands."

I took my palms from her shoulders and put them about three inches in front of her face. I felt her breath on my fingertips before I gradually moved my hands upwards, past her forehead, over her hair and back to the base of her skull. I hadn't touched her head, yet sensed that her right side, particularly at the temple, was much colder than the left. I began to move my right hand in circles above her head as I suggested in a low, slow voice that she relax and absorb the soothing, healing warmth as though she were a sponge, just as I'd learned in my first self-hypnosis class years before.

I moved my right hand to the base of her skull and cupped it very gently as I continued to make circular movements in the air above her head with my left. I worked several minutes and then tested the temperatures at her temples. Now they seemed nearly equal. I felt the rhythm of her breathing in me, and I relaxed completely into the sound of my own voice that was so much different in depth than my normal speaking tones. My relaxation suggestions were affecting both of us. I was aware that there was a silence about us, but we seemed to be in a different place that was a slower plane, joined in some indefinable union that benefited us both. I was resonating with her as though we were two attuned instruments in an unseen orchestra, and I felt a deep sigh arise from the depth of me; I knew somehow that her pain was gone, completely gone. I felt unutterably tender and loving toward this woman. I told her that *she* had the power to let go of her pain, now and in the future, that she had the ability to relax and the knowledge of the way to be painfree.

I opened my eyes and felt misplaced. Others had come to stand behind the people at our table, and no one said a word for what felt like a very long time. The air seemed dense, until Sandy opened her eyes and said in a shocked, abrupt voice, "My headache...the pain...it's gone!"

Then, questions...and the peace in me stayed and allowed me to speak as I'd never been able to answer before.

"We *all* have far more power than we know," I began slowly. "If we wish, we can all sensitize our hearts and our hands to feel the vibrations or energy of others. But when we attune ourselves, we are dealing with a different set of laws of a far different order than that which we use in our practical, everyday world.

"I can tell you a bit about what just happened; if you're willing to suspend judgments, at least for a few minutes, then perhaps the rest will be easier to accept.

"If I were to ask you to describe your immediate reality here in this room, each of you would have a different perspective. One might notice the table setting, another our physical appearance, another the furnishings and dimensions of the room. If we were to compare notes, it would be evident that we all were telling the truth but we each see different *aspects* of reality. We could go on for hours, giving more details of our visible surroundings and still not have any awareness of the invisible basic substance that underlies all the surface appearances.''

I paused for a sip of coffee and continued. ''We and everything here—even inanimate objects—are composed of energy, of matter, that is in constant movement. You may think this mahogany table is solid, but a physicist could tell you that it's composed of the basic building blocks of nature—atoms—and that most of the atom is just empty space with particles whirling around the nucleus, or center. The size of the nucleus to the atom has been compared to a pin in a football field. There is *nothing* that is solid. Not here, not anywhere. Since all life is composed of atoms, *everything* is in movement, whether we see it or not. Nothing is solid.''

''I don't see what that has to do with her headache,'' someone said.

''It has everything to do with pain and wellness. The point of mentioning physics is that once we accept that the world is fluid, not fixed, we begin to grasp that *everything is constantly changing*. The key word is FLUID. In this molecular reality, energies are exchanged, not confined to forms. This is the opposite of a fixed, rigid world: WE INTERACT! I can influence through my energy field—my beingness—my neighbor, this room, our world.

''I can use that energy for high purposes or low, but I DO have power and it is dependent upon my *intent* as to how it's used.

''So, although we can't see it, this energy exists. In this other dimension, I visualize that the energy flows as does water: from higher to lower; out of fullness to nourish that which is lacking. I don't believe the basic transfer requires unusual powers, although some do it more easily and do transmit far more than others.''

''Well, what did you actually DO?'' someone asked.

''First, I centered myself. Each of us can visualize this in a personal, unique way. I take a few deep breaths and imagine my spinal column as a rod of light, coalescing and illuminating the energy that's in me. I'm recharging it by condensing it, and I'll redirect it out through my hands and voice. Some healers actually see an aura radiating from the body; it is, they tell me, a continual light show, an aurora borealis, indicating by its clarity and ever-changing colors the shifting emotional and physical states of the person to be healed. I don't see auras, much as I'd like to. Perhaps some day I'll have that ability.

"But there are other ways of sensing; actually we're all senders and receivers of energy, and to be in a sensing mode is to be quiet, centered and passive, setting the intent to feel what is present in the other without judging it or altering anything. That is, there are no intellectualizations going on in me in that receptive mode: what is in Sandy, *just is.*

"I felt a difference of temperature from one side to the other. If I feel cold, I sense a lack of circulation, a loss of energy, just as my feet might get cold if I'm overtired, anxious, or out of balance. The body always reflects the mental state, and if there is chronic imbalance, symptoms of pain or distress manifest in any of a thousand ways.

"I shift to the sending, or active mode once I've determined where the imbalance is. In Sandy's case, I didn't do a thorough job—I didn't scan the whole body, but sent energy just to her head and neck. If this had been an appropriate time and place, I would have done more.

"Our energies united; for a moment we were one person, not two bodies. When I sighed deeply in relief, I knew *her* pain was gone. In this oneness there is a kind of loving, because for that brief moment there was no longer Sandy and Bobbie, but a merging of a part of us. You see, the teacher who told me about the laying-on of hands taught me that we don't end at our skin. Our bodies know this, even if our rational minds deny it.

"But this presents problems too, and exerts a pull on our entire lives: our reality, always shifting, is constantly influenced by others for good or ill. Our awareness, composed of the seen and unseen, is filtered through the belief system of our limiting mind. The mind limits because it cannot comprehend the vastness of all that is; it defines the world by what it sees and believes, and, by assuming that we are less than we can be, sets that tone, that limitation.

"If the mind is free of the boundaries of thought, it senses more than it consciously knows; in stillness, uncontaminated by mind chatter or directed thought, the self—the body and spirit—feels a sense of order and generosity and peace in the cosmos and in ourselves.

"The very attempt to explain creates limits that are not there. In the freeing of the self from the constraints of language or mind, the 'not-knowing' in the rational sense becomes 'all-knowing' in the depth of our being—in our very bones. If, even for a moment, you have ever tasted that utter bliss of peace and one-ness in a world that is mutable and energized by a sense of the unity of all things, to return to this world of tangibles, you return with a mind that knows that this provable, rational, scientifically oriented world we live in *is not all there is.*

"See, 'healing' is the healing of the self, and it is a never-ending task we face constantly because we're all made vulnerable by our thoughts, by stress in the world ranging from subtle pollution to outright violence. But we CAN listen to our bodies, and do our very best to send harmonious rather than divisive energies out into the world. We can remain open to wisdom that is sometimes inexplicable and can't always be proven by scientific experiments. We're beginning to discover what many other cultures know: tangible energy is present in thought as well as action; it radiates from a deep Source within us that resists definition, and it can be used as a beneficial power to heal ourselves and others, if we make that choice."

I hadn't meant to speak so long, but no one had moved.

As I lifted my cup to drink the cold coffee, I heard quiet voices saying, "Thank you....so much!" from around the room.

Necklace

By 1980, Larry had acquired several large accounts in Hawaii and needed to set up a complex data processing office for the torrential flow of information that had to be transmitted to his computer center in Houston. He loved traveling to Hawaii. The early morning jogs on the beach, late afternoon swims, and casual attitude and dress of his business contacts there, helped to balance the more frequent trips to the eastern United States.

While he worked, I could relax—as long as I stayed out of the sun. My fair, freckled skin just couldn't take it anymore, so I brought books and a typewriter to make use of the hours I was alone. The undemanding silence of a maid-serviced hotel room overlooking the Pacific was a renewal, a reprieve from a busy life. In the evening, if we entertained business associates, I enjoyed the low-key restaurants. Most of all, I needed to spend time with Larry anywhere I could. Our marriage had hit some rocky spots lately, and I attributed it to his constant travel and my increasing loneliness.

A computer expert who worked for Larry met us at breakfast. I'd met Edna several times before and did not like her at all. She was usually strident and overbearing, and I was secretly pleased to see her looking tired and overweight. She grimaced in pain as she sat down at the table, and looked at us like a red-headed bird with her head tilted at an obviously uncomfortable angle.

"What's wrong?" I asked, smiling politely.

"My goddam neck is killing me," she complained. "I had problems with a sore neck at home, but last night I slept in a draft and it got much worse. The pains go all the way from my shoulder into my head, and I'm in agony. Goddam neck is stiff as a board." She didn't ask me to help her, although the last time we'd met—over a year ago—I'd cured a minor eye problem.

After she spoke of her pain we had a pleasant breakfast. Despite her stiffness she was in rare good humor and showed none of her tendencies to be abrasively tough. I had to admit that part of my dislike was jealousy: she did a terrific job for the company, and never missed an opportunity to remind others of her expertise.

I listened most of the time, unable to participate at the business level but adding humorous comments when I could. I looked around at the billowy, ever-changing clouds, the pigeons strutting and cooing over the crumbs at our feet, and the overfed, wildly dressed tourists stuffing food in their mouths.

We sat for about an hour until it was time for their first appointment of the day. I went upstairs, prepared to begin writing.

When I got to our room on the twenty-fourth floor I felt much more like lying down and meditating. It was lovely to indulge my slightest whim without any time demands nor a telephone to ring, and I arranged pillows on the floor to make myself comfortable. I wondered if I could go back to sleep, feeling a little guilty at my lack of desire to sit down at the typewriter. But last night had been a restless one: if we put on the room air conditioner it was especially noisy; without it the humidity was stifling. I yawned and allowed that if I went to sleep instead of being productive for the morning, no one would ever know.

As soon as I was horizontal I experienced an enormous

surge of energy rather than the relaxed, easy feeling I always got when I lay down to hypnotize myself. It was very odd. Stranger still, the heels of my palms were vibrating with intense heat. My mind seemed to focus like the narrow beam of a powerful searchlight, and the sharp awareness came through that I could relieve Edna's pain—and at a distance. It would be a test to prove that healing was possible without the direct laying-on of hands; that energy could be transmitted through space. The ramifications, if I could do it, were enormous. The possibility of sending healing energies without having to rush to someone's side was staggering. It would be a wonderful gift I could give others.

Then I knew absolutely that I *could* do it.

It did not seem to be egotistical; it was just a knowingness that had never been available to me before. I felt as though I were a powerful engine throbbing with life, waiting to be directed and used.

I lay still for several minutes enjoying the feelings; the only doubt that surfaced concerned Edna's location, because I wanted her cooperation. Like and dislike had no place now. I would transmit the force that was in me.

My first phone call found Larry and Edna. I asked to speak to her.

"What's up?" she asked.

"I feel sure I can help your neck and shoulder. Are you interested?"

"Are you kidding? I'm in terrible pain. Sure I'm interested."

"Do you have a quiet place where you can sit down now?"

"No. Not here. We have a meeting about to begin, and then another one scheduled as soon as this is over. I don't know how long I'll be, but I'll find a place sometime today. Do you want me to call you then?"

"Yes, the Ilikai, room 2439. Will you do three things for me until you call back and I give you more specific instructions?"

"You bet. Anything."

"First, take slow deep breaths and give yourself permission to let go of the pain. Tell your pain it's time to leave. Keep monitoring your breath."

"Got that. What else?"

"Well, I noticed you were wearing a very pretty, heavy gold necklace this morning. Would you mind taking it off?"

"I guess not. Bloody thing cost me a fortune; the bugger is solid gold. I'll zip it in my purse. Sure, I'll take it off if that will help. But why?"

"As soon as we hang up our phones, I'm going to visualize myself rubbing your neck and shoulder. The necklace will get in the way, just as it would if you were here in person. I'm going to focus a lot of energy in that area."

"OK. Thanks. Talk to you in a bit."

I sat down on the blue patterned sofa and looked at my hands. They were still hot and tingling, and seemed pinker than usual. I felt very confident about the whole process of healing at a distance. I acknowledged that I wished to do so ... could do so, and formed the specific intent to relieve pain in Edna and still remain clear from picking up her symptoms.

I became very still. I saw myself putting my throbbing hands on her neck, her shoulders.

Time passed, my hands returned to normal, and I sighed and went to the mini-kitchen to fix myself a cup of coffee.

I didn't hear from her for hours and wondered if she had had second thoughts about the whole project. I was beginning to feel annoyed that I'd wasted my time on her.

The phone rang about two o'clock. "Sorry I didn't get back sooner. The meetings just ended and I've been feeling better. But the strangest thing happened this morning right after you called! As soon as I hung up I put my purse down on a desk and reached up to undo my necklace. Before my hands got to the clasp two of the links in front broke open and the whole thing fell to the floor. Are you sure you're not a witch?"

I was shocked and delighted. What a marvelous, graphic demonstration that energy could be transmitted over a distance!

"Amazing," I said happily. "Anything else?"

"Yeah. Right after that, the pain just disappeared—for about half an hour. But it came back nearly as strong as at breakfast."

"OK. Find yourself a nice quiet corner now and visualize me working on you. Keep giving yourself permission to get rid of the pain."

I lay down and tried to recapture the morning's blast of energy, but now the power was gone, subordinated by my ego's needs to *prove* I could do it again. My inner critic whispered in my ear, "You're making a fool of yourself!" and I tensed involuntarily, knowing it wasn't the way to go on. I began to feel panicky as the minutes slipped by and my body lay rigid and demanding. Who did I think I was, after all? It couldn't be possible—healing at a distance. Only fools believed things like that.

My hands did not pulse, nor could I summon up any image of her. I was like a television set that had been disconnected, and could not turn itself on. I got up, annoyed and frustrated.

She didn't call back.

I saw her the next day and noted that her head no longer was at an angle. "I finally went to the bloomin' hospital and got a cortisone shot. Thanks for giving it a go, anyway."

A day later my hand wrote in large printing that covered a page:

HEALING IS FORGIVENESS

I felt as though a blanket of peace had been laid around my shoulders. For the first time in my life I *knew*, deep inside, that only in forgiveness can the energy change for the body to heal and renew itself.

In these last years, whenever I had forgiven myself for being so much less than perfect, for struggling or failing—when I forgave myself *lovingly* for not being all I could be—then inner doors opened for change to take place. But when I demanded, subtly or overtly, that things be as I thought they *should* be, then the energy was not one of acceptance but of demand; it did not allow for change.

It seemed a wonderful reversal of words to note that healing IS forgiveness, rather than the other way around. Three small words, that allowed worlds to transform.

It was a lesson that would need to be relearned, in an excruciatingly painful test.

PART TWO

PATTERNS

Seeds

I assumed that none of life's passages could alter our love for each other. Neither of us, years later, could pinpoint exactly when our marriage began to crumble.

The seeds must have been there for years before they began to sprout: the soil of our individual life experiences, childhood teachings, the culture that taught us a man should be successful in business at whatever cost; the message that a woman was essentially dependent upon her man. We'd certainly had different roles in life, but they had never conflicted before.

Larry, 53, was caught in the whirlwind of business, excited by the ever-changing, unending battle to earn a living, make his company grow, carve a fine name for himself in the marketplace. I knew he felt if he couldn't make it now, he'd never make it. The financial pressure had been extremely heavy the previous year—his company had nearly gone under. Now he traveled more and more, contacting people to sell his company's insurance programs. Nothing was too much work, no place too far: Alaska, New England, Hawaii, Florida. Intoxicated by the possibilities, by the people, he whirled faster and faster, dropping into bed exhausted at night, rising refreshed each morning to begin another round, like a fighter knowing he can endure, will win. Only I knew how difficult it was becoming for him to let go of business, relax and share time with his family. How could I criticize a man who worked so hard? He had so many business problems. With it all, he'd been so uncomplaining, always maintaining a smile and a positive attitude that put anyone to shame who didn't share his enthusiasm and his dreams.

The business phone calls usually began at 6 a.m., often interrupted meals, and occasionally woke us if we got to bed before eleven. He needed to 'keep in touch' with an awesome number of people, and he was able to keep it all straight like a human computer, recalling every detail. He was unable to acknowledge 'negative' emotions of frustration, disappointment or anger, glossing over them, rushing headlong to the next situation, never looking backwards.

His associates and employees became his family, tightly bound by their loyalty to his talent and endurance; they devoted endless hours to their jobs. I liked most of the people he worked with, both in Los Angeles and in other places that I had visited occasionally. Now that the girls were away at college and I had more time, I wondered if I should work to learn his business. I didn't understand the intricacies of computer programming, did not comprehend the endless problems of selling insurance in a country where every state had individual regulations. Not that I couldn't have done it—I'd just been at the home front. Anything negative I said about business sounded unintelligent or critical.

Larry didn't encourage me to work, so I had more time to pursue my own interests. I became less disciplined and felt that the creative surge was waning. The more I learned about self-care, the less I seemed to honor myself; there was little motivation to exercise, although I knew I should. The knowing did not substitute for the doing.

Larry and I grabbed moments together in the car, dashing somewhere—a ball game or dinner with friends. Occasionally, we made time for an overnight stay in a favorite hotel in Laguna, overlooking the sea. But it was not enough—not for me. Loneliness crept in like the tide.

I felt uneasy, vaguely upset about my life, although I was doing things I enjoyed, married to a man I adored. I blamed the discomfort on various things: the onset of menopause, a silent house without children and their laughter, too little time with the man who'd been the center of my existence for nearly twenty-eight years. I waited hungrily for his phone calls when he was away, and they were always warm, intimate, and loving; he never seemed to be down or discouraged. I went out to classes less at night and felt more tired.

But it was all so vague. I was sure things would get better, that I'd cheer up. A warning voice within me knew I should not be a grouch or a complainer. Larry would never appreciate that. He didn't hear the longing for him—more of him—behind the words, or understand the pain beneath the silences from his once cheerful wife. Only up-beat, positive feelings were allowed, except for obviously distressing situations like my mother's illness. I knew anger wouldn't be tolerated. It never had been. He turned away from me coldly if my voice escalated over anything he had done or neglected to do.

I found myself focusing more on the lacks in my life, and the poison seeped from me like invisible gas. If I were merely sad, he petted me as though I were a small child to be comforted after a minor spill. If I rebelled at his lack of attention, he said calmly, patiently, "I love you. You're my whole life!" How dare I complain about feeling unloved after such statements, said so sweetly? But a dull pain arose in my chest, and words caught in the back of my throat.

He had no desire to look at his feelings or mine. When I demanded that he listen to me, he said, "Anger is useless. It never gets people anywhere." He said it with a smile and changed the subject or turned on television.

Others continued to tell us we were "the perfect couple." We were still loving and touching toward each other, though it seemed to me there was an indefinably different quality to it. I was sure the wellspring of spontaneity was gone, while he denied feeling any differences. I wanted to believe him. But beneath the rosy glow of a successful marriage, part of us simmered at low flame, building up pressures. We did not fake our love; attachments built up over the years still entwined us, held us. We were just not able or willing to explore *all* of our marriage—to see in our depths, our humanness.

At least I got intimations of the banked fires—my automatic writing continued to tell me of pressures in my life I chose not to look at, of a future path bound up with an increasing need for spiritual commitment I was unable to define. The only comfort I found came when a few old friends listened sympathetically.

So Larry and I held each other and touched one another while he continued to deny that there was any rift in our marriage. "Everything is wonderful," he'd say with a glowing smile. "Just give me six more months, honey, and I'll be able to cut down on the travel, and live a normal life." Our pride in each other, our tenderness, obscured any wounds, any sore spots.

The umbilical cord of our marriage had to stretch longer and longer. I felt as though I was putting all the loving into the relationship, that I alone nurtured it in spite of my gnawing discontent. I hurried to please him, as he mentally and emotionally withdrew even when at home. I couldn't appreciate the business demands; he couldn't understand my emotional needs. Once I had seen only beloved similarities between us; now I was frightened at the gulf that widened month by month, and chose not to see that we were on very different paths.

Our improving financial situation was no compensation for loneliness, and "things" no substitute for intimacy. We both knew that—but it didn't help. The more insecure I felt about our future, the more it contaminated the present. The more he discouraged my negative feelings, the angrier I became. The less we shared our doubts and problems, the more we drifted, unable to stop.

We went to a counselor, proclaiming our love and closeness. She sensed a discordant note below the words. We promised to share more 'quality time' with each other.

Nothing changed. I continued seeing the therapist; Larry was just too busy, moving from state to state so quickly his own office sometimes lost track of him. On the days he was in town, he had meetings scheduled night and day. Everything was in a state of flux. He had personnel problems, computer problems; he thought he might sell the business. A thousand things were happening at once. "Six more months, honey, and I'll have it all straightened out."

I no longer believed. I'd heard the words too often.

I was sure he was having an affair with a much younger, pretty employee who'd been at our home several times. The energy between them felt thick, charged with a sexual electricity I hadn't felt in a long time.

Now I was overtly angry, openly crying. He turned, as always, from the anger and was puzzled by my crying. Once more at the therapist's, he denied the affair and any negative feelings toward me, although his lips thinned as he spoke. We sat apart on her sofa, fingers no longer touching.

My problems polluted my work, contaminated the joy in all the things I loved to do. How could I be a healer to others when I was so obviously in need of a healing myself? I did less and less of everything, wondering where the hours went. When I laid my hands on Larry to ease his aches, my hands stayed cool instead of being the hot, healing instruments they'd been.

I continued to see Catherine Bond, our therapist. I told her the truth—as much as I dared touch. I was able to express some of the vast, dark reservoir of fear that my world was crumbling. I felt unutterably guilty that I had such negativity. I'd learned old lessons well: Larry and I had always told each other what a special, beautiful life we had; now I couldn't accept myself when I was unhappy. Perhaps I was only an ungrateful, spoiled wife. Maybe I was going crazy, imagining things that weren't there. It was easier to believe him than to trust my inner voice, a 'spirit guide' that was unacceptable to most people I knew.

My body told me of the depths of the pain by being stiffer and chronically tired. My mind seemed to have lost its ability to concentrate on anything for more than a few minutes at a time. I was unable to enjoy life or to laugh; even the terrible puns that I loved to spring on friends no longer came to mind.

When people told me I "had my act together" more than

anyone they knew, I ached, knowing that it was indeed an "act." In public, my veneer was perfect; in private the laughter and the tears came closer and closer together. The thin wall that separated them felt ready to crack under pressure. I began to stay away from people who didn't know the real Bobbie—the frightened child inside a pretend woman. Very few did. It seemed amazing that the world didn't see my pain, that I could fool all but my best friends. My voice often betrayed me. I heard myself speaking in a high, thin, quivery voice without humor.

I raged and cried at Larry, at myself, trying to understand why I was no longer enough for him. Where had I failed?

It was so easy to blame Larry. He was so rarely there, so ready to discount my feelings, to turn away or go to sleep. But when I scanned myself with a cold, critical light, I was sure I was suddenly too old, too sad, too possessive, too jealous, too demanding. I wove a cocoon of negative feelings about our marriage, even as he wove threads of growing indifference.

I made an effort to stop the anger and tears, or at least discharge them when he wasn't around. I became angry at myself for being angry: a Catch-22 of emotions that was not vented by punching the bag I'd set up in the garage. I started out slugging away, imagining Larry's face on the canvas, but ended picturing my own. The effort left me exhausted.

I tapped every resource I'd learned in the easy years, but nothing was as it had been. I meditated, but found no peace. I photographed, and saw no joy. Books were a bore, and food turned my stomach. I wrote, and disbelieved the words.

The first time he said, "Perhaps we'd better separate... you know, to find out how much we mean to each other," was April, 1980, in the midst of one of our now-frequent fights.

I couldn't believe it; in spite of our problems, we were a team—a great team that had fallen on bad times. Surely we would recover if we could only get to the bottom of our troubles.

I was certain I couldn't live without him.

I held fast to Catherine's help, thankful I'd found a wise and loving therapist. She said, "Bobbie, if you only *believed* what you're writing, you wouldn't need any help from me."

When I asked Paul what to do with my doubts and fears, the reply was:

Honor them. Bow to them and salute them, for they are logical and real, but they are not all the truth, not even the largest part of the truth. The truth is in you and begs to be known, and I tell you it, and you may believe or not:

The way is not easy and is purposefully so, for if it were then everyone of faint heart and little belief would walk the same path and do little work. The truth is hard, although the Light shines for everyone if they will but look for it.

And you do look and walk the path in pain now, and it is all right to be in pain. Pain is the fire that brings the Light and separates those who will see from those who will not. I tell you this not to make it easier but to let you know this troubled time shall pass.

And the truth and the soul of you are beautiful, and to be in touch with this you need only BE. The more fight you put up, the longer will be the transition, but the transition is beginning already, although you do not know it in your mind.

Do know that it is your destiny to let this man go— and I tell you he will someday be there for you more than he has been. The change will come, but do not lean on it, for he is in no condition to be there for anyone. He will not now change enough, give enough.

Glory in your anger and your love. Give where you can and what you can, and know you will not suffer more than you can carry.

The golden Light becomes you and is in you. This be no dream—this be real for you, and you be in the right place at this time.

Whom to believe? No one.

I wallowed in doubt and self-pity, wavering between Larry's denials and Paul's affirmations, feeling like a battered child.

By June, Larry and I were avoiding any unnecessary contact. We slept in the same bed, and turned away from each other. I felt like a servant when I did his laundry.

I was sure he was involved with the woman I'd suspected, yet he vehemently denied it—"You're crazy," he said. I wanted so much to believe him.

The pain, the bleakness of my life was insurmountable, and began to blot out everything else. What had I done to deserve this? What was wrong with me? How could I get rid of the pain? I wanted Larry to suffer too, but he seemed to sail through his days, which—incredibly—had become even busier.

By the end of June, I found proof of his affair. My chest felt like an open wound, bleeding and raw. There was no way to close it, to heal me. I was too weak. There was only one man who could do it, who had the power, and he had abandoned me.

We were at war, in silence. At last, in guarded words, he said, "I need to be alone. I don't know who I am, what I want, where I'm going; I don't even have the time to look for an apartment. It looks as though I've got some important companies interested in buying the business."

"Can you wait until after my birthday in September? I just don't want to face that alone," I said, like a child.

"I guess so. I won't be around much anyway."

So we agreed to separate. It was suddenly obvious, inevitable.

Surrender

I could eat little. I lost ten pounds in a matter of days. I wandered around our beloved home like a ghost.

At the nadir of desolation, my father called and said that mother was slipping away. She had withered to about seventy pounds, fifty less than her trim figure when she'd been well. She had begun refusing food, and since she could no longer speak, no one knew why. It seemed she was, perhaps, conscious enough to use the only power she had left. My mother was starving herself to death. My mind filled with images of the concentration camps.

Larry neither held me nor consoled me.

Dad had said she might last for several weeks—perhaps a month. We had such a close, loving relationship, I knew he was puzzled that I didn't fly to be with him immediately, but I'd told him nothing of my marital problems because he was barely able to function with all of his own worries. Now I could no longer pretend that all was well with me. I made excuses, telling him I'd be up in a week.

I didn't have the strength to fly to her. I could barely walk to the bathroom.

Before, I'd cried. Now I was hysterical. I couldn't control gulping, gut-wrenching sobs. The awful weight of my life closed in on me after the phone call, and I sank to the floor in a heap next to my side of our bed, screaming in anguish and torment, begging God for help, for an answer, for a way out.

I raged and sobbed, pounding the floor and the bed in agony, not caring whether I lived or died. I had no idea how long I stayed in that tormented state, the growing pile of used tissues a tattered mess next to me.

When I had no more strength, when exhaustion overtook fury, something miraculous happened. From the abyss of my despair, I suddenly came into possession of reasons, of answers. I was afraid I'd lose it. Something in me had changed, I was sure. I grabbed the newsprint pad I kept under the bed and began to write, still crying, knowing I had to capture the feelings and the wisdom before I forgot, before misery blotted out memory.

July 1, 1980. My mother is dying of starvation. It's a question of time—weeks, a month, perhaps two. I didn't know I had so many tears.

In my imagination I embrace her and kiss her, lifting the weightlessness of her body. 'Mother,' I say, 'it's peaceful there. You'll be with your mother and father again. Go quietly, without fear. It's golden and loving.'

And I see that I have to let go of far more than my mother for my life to be without fear and have meaning in the deepest sense.

I am making a vow to God: I WILL TRUST, for my needing to possess, to control, has stopped my growth. I realize I've lost the delight of each new day bringing me a surprise. That my holding on to anyone or anything—mother, Larry, my own 'rightness' or 'goodness' IS death, because it kills growing and being. It's no coincidence that the news of mother comes at this time. She is showing me a release.

God, I will give up these people, these things, because I know, deep within me, it's necessary to go unencumbered by that heaviness of needing and possessing. I know I need help.

Something in me knows that homage by the mind without the spirit is no homage at all. These endless tears are the visible signal of a great, walled-up dam in me that is breaking apart and releasing fears. No wonder I haven't been creative in this last year and a half. I've cheated myself out of BEING FULLY WHO I AM—in agony now, in joy some other time. I've cheated Larry out of the beauty of me, by deflecting to him what I could not admit was my own lack of trust in God, and in myself.

But I feel, through these tears, that I NEEDED this anger, this jealousy, this lack of trust, this controlling energy that has debilitated me in so many obvious and subtle ways—I needed this part of me so I could LEARN from it, SEE IT AS A PART OF MY BEING—as a worthwhile piece, because it has, like a volcanic eruption of pain, forced me to look at what I have not been willing to see.

Thank you for preserving my body during this terrible time, for keeping me safe to undergo this. Thank you for giving me a loving father who can feel, and cry, and share his life with me, and for my wonderful children, whom I've let fly away.

Thank you for giving me this soul, this spirit, this being—which, while stubborn, still can respond.

And thank you for Larry, as imperfect as I—but in different ways. I thank you, God, that he—that we— in anger and in love, have come to this painful point in our lives.

I trust you to take care of us.

The miracle is that those things that I've hated in

myself were my friends, as Catherine said, because they've brought me to this point as surely as they could. Not quickly, but through a path that I needed to travel.

I thank you, God, for my unfaithfulness to you and for Larry's to me, for they have brought me to this mountaintop where at last I can see where I've been. I didn't learn from my ego trips before, so I guess I need to go through this.

Thank you, mother, for allowing me to see in the loss of you, the strength of you. Once, I blamed you for my faults. Now I see how I came to need them. Oh, my God, my God, the dam in me only broke when I held my mother and offered her to you in your time and hers: NOT IN MY TIME. I see me so clearly, picking her up and loving her and rocking her and kissing her, and BEING HER AND BEING ME AT THE SAME TIME AND LETTING HER GO. And suddenly she is gone and I hold Larry tightly but freely and love him and love me not less and you a little more and he is free and I am free and we love again as two children who come together to play in the sunshine. And we are.

Go—all of you—and come back when you wish, how you wish. I will know your touch.

Separation

Mother began to eat. Her weight never again went above eighty pounds, but she would live for another two years.

The incredible feeling of release during my 'surrender' seemed to go underground, to some secret vault that kept records without bringing them into the daylight for scrutiny. I looked at the words I'd written, remembered the pain and the sudden freedom of trusting rather than fearing...but no miracle occurred that I could see. Slow, tiny changes, perhaps: I began to sleep a bit more, eat a little, but I was afraid to open to what I could not see—and all I could see was misery. I felt as though I had died and been reborn to witness my own suffering.

Cathy and two dear friends urged me to move out, to find an apartment somewhere and get away from Larry. I had never thought of it, and dismissed the idea as impossible. HE wanted the separation; HE was moving out. I would stay at home. It was inconceivable that I could abandon it as he'd abandoned me.

The idea persisted, much as I tried to squelch it. I was shocked to realize I'd never lived alone. I'd gone from childhood home to university to marriage without a pause.

Perhaps—just perhaps—I was being self-indulgent, probing my wounds with a pointed tongue because the terrain was so very familiar. I'd been feeling so negative for so long that a radical step might be the only answer. It felt like a big risk, yet a small stirring began in me, and the thought of 'getting out' gave me some fresh food for my mind and emotions instead of the familiar carousel of bad feelings.

The idea began to seem possible. Denise, home from school for summer vacation, and utterly shocked at the disintegration of family and home, thought I should move. Cathy suggested that the change was not running away, but a positive step towards a new beginning. I began to think that perhaps depression would not follow me.

Larry and I had always wanted to live near the water, and it seemed especially calming and inviting now; I could take long walks by the sea, get away from the heat and smog in the valley.

I soon found a place I liked in Mariner's Village, a lush, huge complex of apartments near the ocean in Marina del Rey. The unfurnished one-bedroom apartment was tiny but attractive, and required a six-month lease.

I felt an unfamiliar blast of courage, and came home to tell Larry. I needed his signature to guarantee the rent.

"I need to talk to you," I said. "Could you please come into the living room?"

"I'll be there when this program is over."

I needed to compose myself, to hide the sudden fear that he'd make me stay in our house, alone, like a musty housekeeper with no job but tending the ancestral property. He'd said HE wanted to move out. Now I did.

I heard the television click off. He walked into the room and sat down across from me. I watched him attentively, unexpectedly recalling what I'd learned about body language years ago.

"You wanted to speak to me?" he asked calmly.

"Yes. I found an apartment. I need to move away from here."

He quickly crossed his legs and folded his arms across his chest. I was sure his eyes changed color.

"You what?" His voice was still calm, his body rigid.

"I'm going to move away from this place, these memories of us. And I need your signature on the lease."

"You do?"

"I do. The apartment will be vacant in a month. I can move on September 25th. I'll leave everything here for you except for the white chaises and a table. It has a refrigerator. OK?"

"OK."

"Are you surprised?"

"No. No. Not at all, sweetheart." Same old Larry, denying everything that makes him less than cool, collected, and in control.

I thought: who is the real Larry? I'm fighting for my life, and he's saying 'sweetheart' as though he still loves me and nothing has happened.

The next day we signed the lease for my apartment. Both of us, in a tiny surge of our old togetherness, held hands as we looked at all the boats sailing to the ocean. Some of our happiest times had been spent racing the small boat he'd built in the garage, never believing his lack of handiness could bring forth anything that floated. Eight months of evening work after his job—proudly, he'd named it after me. None of our friends had been able to understand our joy in spending every Sunday in a cramped, open sailboat battling the waves and wind, laughing as we lost each race to better sailors. Once he'd said, pointing at the complex into which I'd be moving, "someday when the kids are grown, I'd like to live right there." And here I was, moving in alone and wondering what happened to the dream along the way. It sounded like a corny movie plot.

"I'll come and visit a lot, if you'll let me," he said wistfully. "We'll have breakfast together, and I'll jog by the water. You'll see—we'll be back together in six months, honey. I just need time."

The loving words were somehow as painful as the harsh ones. Oh, please, God, I thought. Just a few months more, and maybe we'll be back together. Tears filled me again, and I turned away to walk to the car.

He pulled me back by the hand. "I'm so sorry, honey." I believed him . . . and it didn't help at all.

Alone

My mind reeled with moving plans.

I had always surrounded myself with so many things: books, pictures, clothes, plants. Now I wanted a bare minimum. The hope flickered like a pilot light that I'd be back in my home again soon...that moving out would be a short, bad dream. In the meantime, the small apartment would hold very little.

The big problem concerned beds.

I felt I needed to fill 'all' of a bed: I'd been half of a king-sized one for so many years, I was sure I'd feel lost if I moved ours and slept in it alone. Besides, what would Larry use? I refused to acknowledge that he might sleep elsewhere. Anyway, when he traveled, we still needed a bed for the house sitters. So I determined to take the twin beds from Linda's and Denny's rooms. I bought some new sheets to mark a new start.

"What are you going to do if a man wants to spend the night?" Ely asked.

"I'm not interested," I said. My heart stirred like a wounded animal when I thought I might never want anyone, or—worse—no one might want me.

"Bobbie, you can't know what's going to happen. I think you're *crazy* to take twin beds. Do you like making love in such a cramped space?"

"No," I said, remembering vacation hotels. "But I'm not moving down there to make love to anyone. I don't even like ME right now. Besides, I've bought all the linens."

"Take them back. I've got a king-sized mattress in the garage that my son isn't using since he bought a waterbed, and you can borrow it. Please...trust me."

Moving day went smoothly, even though I came down with a cold.

Larry called and invited me to lunch the following day. The girls sent some beautiful flowers with a card that read, "We love you, mom, and we're with you." I cried and put the card in my wallet.

In the beginning, it was all a bit like being in a playhouse. The kitchen was so small I never had to take a step to use sink, refrigerator or stove. The tiny bathroom was poorly planned; I didn't have room to brush my teeth or get out of the shower if the door was open. The bedroom was tolerable, and the living room had a lovely stone fireplace with gas jet and logs; when the fog rolled in and the day turned damp and chilly, I could curl up with a book, turn on some music, and feel as though I was in a cozy, protective nest awaiting the return of my prince.

Reality returned when everything had been put away. Everything was mine, all right: no man's clothes anywhere. No television blaring a ballgame, no man's mess in the kitchen. And no one at all in the king-sized bed in which I still slept on the right half, telling myself it was so much easier to make up in the morning than messing up the middle.

I raced up and down on a roller coaster of emotions: fear of the unknown, excitement at new possibilities, pleasure in my own company, terror at the loss of husband and home, wonder that my life had changed so drastically. Above all and below all was anger at Larry for 'doing it,' for being with someone else and lying about it. He was never at home when I called.

Old habits persisted. If I was out in the late afternoon, I'd find myself rushing home to fix dinner. It was only when I unlocked the door and looked around that I realized I had no one to fix it for. I usually ate leftovers from lunches that were suddenly too big.

Once or twice a week I went to our home to retrieve a kitchen or clothing item I'd forgotten, sit on the floor with Moose and cry at the memory of the three of us playing in the park. She licked tears from my cheeks, wagged her tail, and ran for a tennis ball for me to throw. I didn't want to play any more.

Larry's business was sold the week after I moved. Life was so capricious—by some crazy twist of fate, now that we no longer had each other, we had no more money problems. Had he been offered a chance to go back in time, to simpler, closer, years, I knew he'd not be willing to give up the triumphs of battles won in the marketplace. And I? Would I be willing to let go of the joys I'd glimpsed—the possibilities—in my moments of psychic clarity and intuitive knowledge? It hadn't harmed our marriage, of that I was certain. After healing had cured his elbow, he'd been fine with all that. But if it *had* contributed in some way to our split, I couldn't make myself say that I'd have given it all up to be with him.

There must be life after Larry, I thought. I began to check into classes and seminars so I'd have less time to sit in the apartment and brood.

Two weeks later I was in a five-day, experiential workshop that was to prove an important breakthrough in many ways.

I began by feeling utterly alone; I barely knew the person who'd recommended it. But I'd been in so many classes by myself with no fears—I was sure it was only because each night I had to go home through a dangerous part of town, park in a poorly lit garage near my apartment in an area known to be ripe for robberies, and fall asleep by myself, sharing nothing with no one.

The workshop dealt with the feelings I had, in a very constructive way; it was far more than just a lecture alone could have been. At the close, I felt warm, loving and surrounded by friends... able to handle life. I was suspicious that the joy might not last, but at least I'd met some interesting people who knew me as an individual and not half of a team. We promised each other a reunion party.

I saw Cathy as before—once a week. She was a constant source of support and awareness, never minimizing my feelings, but encouraging me to discover new options. One day she said, "Bobbie, I think we need to discuss your ideas about a relationship."

"Well...I'm not ready. I guess I'm even more scared than disinterested; in this age of sexual permissiveness, I must be a real misfit—I've never slept with another man. That felt like a plus when I was married, but I don't even know what to do now. Here I am, forty-eight years old, and I know I'm not planning to go to bars. I don't handle liquor well, and the last thing I want to do is get loaded and end up in bed with some stranger."

"That's fine—to know what you *don't* want to do. I just want to mention that you're very vulnerable right now. You don't need another rejection, and some men have a way of sensing that in a woman and can take advantage of it. I'm not trying to scare you...I just want to make you aware of it. What I'd rather discuss is what you DO want in a man. If you had any and all wishes gratified, what would they be?"

I thought a long time before I answered; I hadn't focused on my desires in a long time. My actions had all been defensive. I fidgeted on the sofa, and said at last, "Well, this is going to sound strange. It even feels funny *thinking* about it, but I'd like someone younger than me, someone who's the direct opposite of Larry. I mean, I don't want a businessman in a hurry, I don't care about traveling right now, and money can't buy me anything I really want. There isn't anything I do *want*. But I have to admit, I'm tired of endless business phone calls, and I don't care about big deals." I felt stronger and more positive, and added, "In fact, I'd like someone who shares *my* interests—photography and healing... and music and books. I want someone who's sensitive and tender, and not afraid of showing a feminine side. And what the hell—I want a fantastic lover, too.''

I laughed at the absurdity of it all, and Cathy joined me, saying, ''I think that's great. He sounds rather like a late-blooming hippie; I don't know any of those, but I hope you get exactly what you asked for. Keep your eyes open!''

I left the appointment feeling lighter, just a bit silly, and very surprised at the description that had poured out of me. I just didn't know anyone who fit it.

I had a late afternoon appointment with a dermatologist. I'd developed a couple of funny little growths on my face and tip of my nose, and I wanted to have them removed. He took one look at me, and said, ''I'm going to biopsy three of your spots. I'm quite sure they're malignant. And I'm concerned about the one on your nose—if it is what I think, you'll need some plastic surgery to repair the dent I'll have to leave.''

I was shocked. I felt very resentful of another burden on my already tight shoulders, and the tension from his discussion, scrapings and shot left me with runny eyes, a tender nose, and a foul mood. I drove home an hour later, wishing I had a cave to hide in and a club to wield at the world.

Unfortunately, I'd invited someone over whom I'd met at the workshop, and seen once since, along with an old friend. I couldn't remember his last name, or where he worked. I wanted to tell him—to warn him—to stay away, but I had no way of reaching him. At least I hadn't invited Richard to dinner. I hadn't cared enough to do that.

The doorbell rang promptly at 7:30. ''What happened to you?'' he said, looking at the band-aids on my face.

My nose still hurt and I couldn't think of anything witty to say, so I motioned him to come in and asked, ''How about a glass of wine?'' before he sat down.

''Sure.''

I poured one for each of us, and tried to look interested as he began speaking of his attempts to get a job with the Los Angeles County Museum of Art as a photographer.

We talked and drank; I was tired and hoped the evening would end at an early hour, but conversation seemed easy and unforced, although my mind was never far from the doctor's diagnosis, and wine only dulled the edges of the worry.

Richard seemed a likeable man, rather solitary in his frequent retreats to the high desert country. I was surprised to hear that he, too, was studying acupressure.

He obviously was unimpressed with the musical selections I'd been playing on the stereo. "Do you mind if I look through your records and find something else?" he asked.

"No. I don't have many in this apartment, though. Everything is in the bedroom—there just wasn't enough room in here." I carried my wine with me and put it down on the portable table I used as a nightstand. There were no chairs, so we sat on the edge of the bed, talking about the abstract serigraph—my favorite artwork—that hung over the stereo and record player. He got up to change the record, and sat down again, slightly nearer to me than he'd been before. I felt uneasy. Part of me wanted to see what it felt like to kiss a bearded, moustached man, and part of me wanted to run back to the living room and sit far apart, as we'd done all evening.

"I'd really like to get to know you better," he smiled, and leaned closer.

"Yes," I said, just before he kissed me. I had no idea it could feel so good.

We kissed and kissed. Electric shocks ran up and down my spine. I felt as though the woman who was responding so quickly to this stranger was someone who had been hiding inside me for a very long time.

We eased gently into a prone position on the bed. He began stroking my back. I didn't want him to stop, but I began to panic: what would I do if he wanted to make love? I couldn't just peel off my clothes. I'd be too embarrassed—and anyway, I'd have to take precautions against getting pregnant. Should I come out in a sexy nightgown? A robe? Nothing? Suppose he didn't want to make love after all, and suddenly got up and left?

"I really want to make love to you," he said.

"Oh, yes," I answered, and got up weakly.

"Do you have any candles and incense?"

I told him where they were, locked myself in the bathroom, and heard a new record being played. I panicked: how much time should I take? I thought. Should I shower? Just put on perfume? Would I look funny to him? It took all my strength to open the door.

Two candles were flickering at either side of the bed. I could smell incense smoldering and perfuming the room. Music was throbbing at low volume. He was on my side of the bed under a sheet, and I fell quickly into bed next to him, praying he'd not noticed my imperfect body, old surgery scar, and nervous smile.

He was very tender and very loving as he resumed kissing and stroking me. I felt him huge and hard against me, and I wanted him inside, as much as I'd wanted anything in a very long time.

I loved the softness of his beard, the feel of his silky skin. I was positive I reeked of too much wine turned sour and inexperience made visible.

When morning came, after a long, intense night, the face I saw reflected in my mirror was pale green, freckled and dotted with band-aids. He would be turned off, I was sure. Who would want a woman who looked as old as I did? He was only thirty-seven, after all, and could have his pick of women.

He was tired, unwilling to go to work, and oblivious to my infirmities.

I wondered if I'd ever see him again. I couldn't eat the food I'd felt obligated to fix him for breakfast. I tried pretending I didn't have a hangover, but it didn't work. I did.

"Want to go to a movie this weekend?" he asked as he kissed me goodbye.

"Yes," I said, once again.

Resistance

I walked by the boat channel to the breakwater that jutted out to sea, attempting to understand the changing patterns of my life.

I felt like a jigsaw puzzle with the pieces not yet together; I was sure if I just had more patience, I'd have a complete picture. The edges were set, but there were large gaps in the interior.

I tried—that forbidden, tainted word—to think through the recent events, but I couldn't maintain continuity of thoughts and feelings for very long. I'd suddenly become exhausted, and the new pieces, so close to being put in place, dissolved in my imagination. I was left holding the old ones, pieces I didn't enjoy looking at: an over-protected, only child grown into an emotionally dependent woman, one who needed to make her husband perfect and maintain an image of an unblemished marriage. It added up to failure—after all, if I'd been the wonderful wife, mistress, companion, friend, mother, that I thought I'd been, that I'd tried to be, then I wouldn't be walking alone. There must be something wrong with me.

On an overcast, dreary day, with foghorns bleating in the distance, I walked quickly, anger building again. I began to play with the idea of *resistance*, as though it was a heavy ball that had a special weight and density. I didn't want to look at it, but my resistance to dealing with resistance seemed humorously on target; I was like a moth trying to avoid the flame, yet being pulled nearer by my flutterings. I had another low-grade infection that sapped me of vitality, and I had the feeling Paul might have some pertinent advice. I turned back on the path, attempting to get a fix on what he'd say, unable to form a thought. He wrote:

> *The internal process always manifests itself in terms of health or disease.*
>
> *The silent growth of resistance at low levels has crept in like moss upon a tree and this engenders infections that do not incapacitate but undermine the mental and spiritual bodies and cause small physical changes.*
>
> *When you cannot accept controlling or fearful aspects of the self, then resistance sets in. It is one of the most corrosive forces known, for it gives little warning, is a silent force, and is disguised by many other states which are labelled "good" or "bad."*
>
> *Resistance is a stealthy polluter of the spirit, of energy, of beingness, for it lives in dark places and is covert. Even procrastination is obvious compared to it. The manifestation of resistance is all the things you fear: anger, jealousy, rage...and fear itself. The resistance is that YOU ARE AFRAID OF LETTING GO. The parents trained you to be nice and proper and to be acceptable to others. You will be all these things and many more, if you but let go of the need to be them.*
>
> *You have been resisting yourself—all the parts of yourself. It is time now for your renaissance.*

I felt like an old book being illuminated by a new light.

Relationships

The biopsies were negative.

The relationship filled a need in each of us. Richard and I were two lonely people desperately yearning to give and receive loving. He'd also been deeply hurt in a recent relationship and could easily understand my fears of being rejected again. We each needed to find someone to trust, to share the gains and losses of our lives. We found our trust in each other came slowly, not purchased with sexual intimacy alone. We built it on cold nights in a warm bed with words when passion was done.

"Look into my eyes," he'd say. "I need to see your eyes." He tried to test me to see if I was lying as others had done. Then, satisfied I was not, "What do you want from me?"

I craved what he also wanted: loving, and a caring relationship that would not tolerate any lies, small or large. We promised nothing, and in the void that promises think to fill, we found a deep regard for each other that was friendship and sexuality—an oasis of comfort and pleasure. We were not possessive of each other and made no demands of exclusivity nor 'foreverness.'

In Richard I found an exquisitely sensitive, playful, passionate lover. He set the scene for our lovemaking with candles and incense, lighting and music. He introduced me to sensuality at many levels: often, before making love, we meditated. It cleared away the day's tension, and opened our hearts to the pleasure that would come afterwards. We sat crosslegged in front of the fire, holding hands, sending energy coursing between us, lost in our private world of balancing ourselves and gratitude for having found another with whom to share such a healing ritual. Time stood still as we opened to our own, and each other's unfolding.

He found in me a loving, tender companion who shared the pathways of his spirit. What I had so blithely asked for, I had indeed received. The generosity of the gift that had been bestowed was not lost on me. Each day I marveled that I was healing and opening at the same time.

Richard cared little for money, possessions, competitiveness. He introduced me to sleeping in a van on a desert plateau, rock concerts, and daily prayers of gratitude for one's existence.

I, on the other hand, was willing to learn, but unwilling to let go for long of physical comforts and convenience. I thought we were a perfectly wonderful 'odd couple,' each supplying what the other lacked, and never destined to make of our relationship anything which bound us too tightly.

We each needed freedom, but in different ways. He required frequent backpacking trips to lonely places that kept his lean body in shape and his soul refreshed. I wanted emotional space to find out who I really was after all the years of marriage and parenting.

In music, meditation and lovemaking with Richard, I began to realize that the singles world I'd been forced into was one that had its rewards—not the ones I'd treasured, such as stability and predictability, but a sense of excitement and the assurance that I was, after all the self-denigration, still an interesting and desirable woman.

Occasionally I dated others and enjoyed their company, finding that I had an untapped capacity for friendship with men as well as women.

Larry and I continued to see each other, usually once a week for dinner. The breakfasts and jogging at the beach never materialized. He did not spend a night.

We were friends and enemies, and could not disentangle the web of our lives.

He would knock at the door of my apartment, stand back to admire the way I looked, hold me in a long and loving embrace, glance wistfully at the warm fire and cozy room, sit down, and begin drinking and talking. Eventually, we'd get to dinner.

One night, after watching me over a glass of wine, he said, "God, I love you." His eyes brimmed with tears. "Are we going to make it?"

"I don't know." I made myself remain calm, while questions screamed in my head—questions I'd asked before, questions that brought me down in dark, deepening circles.

If I had said to him, "If you love me, how can you leave me? How can you turn to another woman and let our marriage die?" it would have gotten us nowhere. He couldn't have answered, because he was a man torn apart, denying his new love and claiming he was lonely. He was still attached to me and struggling to be free, evidently not wholly committed to his new life. He was filled with remorse, consumed with guilt, and could not let either of us go. With agile charm he danced between us, but the speed of his life could not outrace his emotions, which apparently were working closer to the surface.

After such a draining 'date,' I felt like a shipwreck victim, trying to float in a dark and turbulent sea. I asked Paul to write after Larry had left.

Please help, Paul. I feel so very strange right now. I want to run away from everything I feel you will write, and that's never happened before. Well, on with it, I guess.

> *You do not wish to know the truth.....the truth is that you selected him for the very reasons that you leave him—not at all the conscious you, the one you know quite well.....but your soul journey has picked this man for these reasons for your lessons in*

*this life, and you are learning well. You have not
failed, and will not.*

*Your life will be filled with great happiness and
laughter and joy in giving. The issue here, as it has
always been, is TRUST. Now you do trust this writing, and now you begin to see how necessary it was,
for without this you would have perished in an emotional sense, and withdrawn to a sad inner world.....
but you do go on and I am here.*

*More, you are fully here now in great distress, and
willing to live until you are through it. This is important. What you do not hear, is that his affairs and this
separation was your decision too, for your growth.*

*The mind of you will never fully accept that, so be
aware it is so, and allow that thought to be there and
do nothing with it.*

*The man in the desert teaches you new ways to deal
with your thoughts, and at this time the release from
the prison of your past experiences and your thoughts
are of utmost concern, and all support systems help.*

Why am I crying now, Paul? Why is this time hearing your
words so different from other times when I haven't cried?
The tears seem slow, and full of infinite sadness.

*They are.....you are correct. You cry for the lost
dreams, the lost love.*

How do I give up my fantasies of getting back together, as
well giving up the man I loved and trusted with my life?

*You do it by letting go of the need for a future that
has a shape you know, and you do it by letting go of
the past and what it was or was not. You become a
child again—tender and loving and vulnerable and
creative and daring, and you do this by letting go of
everything that is not real.*

*The true wonder of this is that you then let go of the
hate and agony for the man, and allow him to work*

out his own destiny. You will not let him go until you give yourself permission to let go of all that has been and all that you think should be. THAT IS THE MESSAGE FOR THIS SOUL TRANSIT.

You have a capacity to know the future, if you but choose to look at it. Not all—that would be a burden more than you could bear.....but you have great wisdom, and it is in this time span of dead leaves that you trust, and this is the ultimate beginning that you have needed. Your years are many, and the life that bubbled so freely returns to you, although there is much slowness in this—but great laughter and joy would not be appropriate at this time.....what is appropriate, and which your body can handle well, is sadness and relief, and the release from the fears of betrayal, for now it has happened and is over.

Exercise the body lovingly and free up the heart, for the rest is here, and you are free to be at one with yourself and the Creator.

IT IS YOUR TIME, IF YOU WILL BUT SEE IT.

Thank you, Paul. You have been my rock.

There were, it seemed, so many Bobbies. I was like an unstable weather pattern: by quick turns sunny, dismal, stormy or calm.

In spite of continued therapy and seminars, a part of me was still very angry and not at all ready to forgive Larry or give up my 'victim' role. What made me work to get out of it—and it took every ounce of energy on bad days—was the example I had of other women I knew who'd turned into shrews after divorce. The world was full of them: women who gave up everything but bitterness. Wallowing in it brought them nothing but a brittle satisfaction in having the last, angry word. Anything...*anything* felt better than that.

On other days, I sang as I drove my car, and noticed that a part of me loved the freedom to do as I wished, when I wished. When I felt peaceful, and thoughts were clear and unmuddied, I realized how little control I had over the future. I was content to live in the present, accept what came, and was surprised at feeling so happy.

I saw little difference between busyness and loneliness; when I felt at peace, being alone seemed a gift of time rather than a penalty for failure. If I fell into a pattern of doubt, of anger, I tended to mask the discomfort by becoming very busy, very hurried, so that I found no time to meditate, to go within to find that I was, after all the turmoil, still whole and complete.

I'd often been told by others, "It's a cruel, mean world out there." Fearful friends had described divorced women who had floundered in the singles world, and then—bruised and rejected—withdrawn into the company of women, hating all men for the damage done by a few.

I'd wallowed in self-pity often enough to read the signs very well: seeing everything that was negative without any attempt to balance it with the positive. The sticky residue of criticism left me angry, usually disguised by an attitude of 'poor me, rotten Larry.' Just when I thought I was done with it forever, it sneaked in for another visit, ended most readily by allowing the newly playful part of me to resurface. The growing ease of the relationship with Richard smoothed the way.

Lucky me. The first time I cooked dinner for him, he offered to help. The kitchen was too tiny for the two of us, so he sat on a stool across from the counter and read poetry while I stirred the vegetables. I wondered that I didn't fall in love with him at that moment, but some inner voice knew that such an involvement would be to fall into the trap of thinking love would bind up all my wounds, instead of doing the healing myself, from within. So we laughed and made love, and it was incredibly, wonderfully restorative.

Linda and Denise were continually supportive and I was amazed at their wisdom and perspective. I could not remember being as mature at their age, although I'd been married when I was younger than they were now. One night Linda asked, "Mother, what was your most terrible fear?"

I answered reluctantly, "That dad would leave me for another woman."

"Aren't you proud of yourself? Look how well you're doing!" Her words and hug warmed me.

Very few saw the dark days, when I was a porcupine curled in a tight ball to ward off the world.

When the crust of anger fell away I still wanted Larry back—the old Larry: playful, funny, and dear. The one I'd married, an eternity ago, not the new, unfathomable executive.

We were drifting farther apart. Once we went away with our best friends, to a place we loved by the sea near Carmel, California. Elly and Maury provided plenty of time for us to be alone, and Larry and I, eternal beachlovers, walked and talked and spoke of a future again as a team. We held hands and spoke joyously of finding a life together, although his future had a non-specific time of arrival, and I dared not antagonize him by reverting to my old demanding self. We did not make love, although we shared the same bed.

After the trip, Larry drove me home from the airport. He quickly dropped my suitcase at the door and left immediately, firmly negating my rekindled hopes for a reconciliation.

Burial

The months passed slowly, a see-saw of changes and the constant pull of decisions. The nights were thick with dreams.

Larry found a place to live in Laguna Beach overlooking the ocean. Three months later, I moved to Santa Monica, nine blocks from the beach. We put our home up for sale, and a friend of Denise's lived there with Moose until I could take the dog in my new, larger apartment.

Larry and I were unpredictable—quick to talk, cry, smile, and fight, but no longer always touching or embracing each other at the beginning and end of each 'date.'

We decided to go to Denise's graduation at the University of Colorado and spend a few extra days alone together after the ceremony in a friend's condominium in Vail.

It was a strange interlude of peace and tenderness. Anyone looking at us would have thought we were honeymooners, so lovingly did we touch and talk and stroll about the town, holding hands and looking at the quaint shops. Each listened intently as the other spoke of feelings. There was not much laughter in us, but a new awareness of the frailty of love and dreams. Hope grew in me like a flower.

We returned home, only to fight the following week: me, in impotent rage; him, in cold fury. We were back to the old pains, the open wounds.

Two months later, we agreed to spend our 29th anniversary together, at a little restaurant in Laguna. We held hands and tried to speak quietly of safe subjects over wine and dinner. I was awash with tears, he with guilt.

The next morning, after a loveless, tormented night, we began to talk haltingly, measuring our words like syrup.

"How much should we see each other?" he asked.

"I don't know," I said, angry at myself for still feeling needy.

The phone rang. While Larry spoke of business matters, I collected the remnants of thoughts and found something new welling up in me.

"I know why I've been so leaky," I smiled.

"What, honey?" He reached out to touch me.

"I'm so tired of *pretending!* Of trying so hard! Let's face it: we just don't have a marriage. Not on any level. Not physically, not emotionally—not even in our goals. I need peace and serenity, and you said last night you want to abandon yourself to business and travel. You can't be a husband to me, and I'm no longer a wife for you. But I miss you so as a friend! I've missed your humor, your sense of silliness, your personality, your...being. I want you to be there for me if I need you, as I'll be for you. But we just aren't making it as a team, and it's been almost a year since we separated." I began to cry again, but this time felt restored, not depleted.

Larry looked surprised and pleased. I had said it for both of us.

He moved closer, and rocked and kissed me. "You're right, honey." We felt the beating of each other's hearts, yet were devoid of passion.

"Let's bury it," he said.

"What?"

"Our marriage. Let's bury it!"

"Yes, let's," I agreed, and we laughed together, relief evident in our voices. He looked at me with appreciation and warmth, eyes crinkled at the corners.

He fixed breakfast for us, a first that caused more laughter. We ate on the porch overlooking the calm sea.

We read the paper, took a walk, went for a swim. I balanced a bank statement of a joint account. He did the washing, another first.

We knew when it was time for the ceremony. He offered me a notepad with LJP stamped in brown, large letters across the top.

"No thanks. Got anything without your initials? No offense," I giggled and found some plain lined paper.

We sat on opposite sides of the room, writing in silence, listing what we were giving up. I wrote slowly, gazing out to sea between patches of words.

I finished, and looked over at Larry, who was looking at me seriously. "You wrote more than I did," he said.

Competitive to the end, I thought. "Does that matter?" Me, picky from the start. Did anything ever change?

"Do you want to go first?" he asked.

"Yes, I'd love to. 'I, Barbara Slote Probstein, do hereby give up:

my jealousy

my possessiveness

my need to make Lawrence Jay Probstein perfect

my need to change him to what I think he should be

my emotional dependency

I also honor the following items:

that I am also responsible for the failure of this marriage

that I am a loving, capable woman who has her own life to lead

that it is my choice to look at this ceremony and what has happened to us as an opportunity rather than a loss.' "

I felt suffused with self-confidence: a new woman who had survived the loss of a love, and come out tempered like fine steel.

He read his paper. He said, "I hereby give up the most wonderful woman a man ever had. I give up feeling guilty at breaking up our marriage, and I promise to love her dearly even if we aren't together."

We kissed and held each other closely for a long time, then walked downstairs hand in hand. We went to the edge of the waves where the sand was moist from the incoming tide and scooped a shallow hole with our hands. He put his paper in; I tore mine to shreds first, as though to protect my promises if the ocean uncovered them.

We mounded sand over the hole. I had no marker to identify the burial.

We kissed again.

"Do you mind if I go for a short swim?" he asked. "I'll be right back."

"Not at all," I smiled lovingly, more relaxed and at peace than I'd been in a year and a half.

He disappeared into the gentle waves as I stared at the little bump on the shining beach. I promised myself I'd honor the vows, even as an ache of loneliness twinged my heart.

Movements

No one who came to my light and airy home ever failed to comment upon the serene quality that had less to do with its architectural beauty and furnishings than a kind of invisible patina left by loving friends and my own daily prayers of gratitude. The white walls reflected rainbows from a high leaded window, and the ever-changing light patterns gave gratitude a daily beginning. Richard had lit a candle and blessed each room in a simple, profound ceremony, and I was sure that, too, had left a peaceful energy.

I knew there were many ways to observe my life. When I could be lovingly detached, I saw myself as privileged to have the opportunity to be forced to grow beyond the boundaries I had set. If I saw myself as alone and rejected, I became a prisoner of memory until I wrenched free by using every tool I had learned, plus acknowledgment that I was a survivor.

I should have realized that nothing with Larry was cleancut or predictable anymore.

In September, about five weeks after our 'burial' ceremony, he took me to dinner a few days before my birthday. He said,

207

"Darling, I know nothing is working for us, but please don't give up on me. I love you, and I know a part of you still loves me despite all the pain I've caused you. I don't want a divorce now, and I don't care how long it takes for us to learn to be together—I'm willing to do that, and I hope you are, too."

He reached for my hands across the table. "I can't pretend I'm over my craziness. I know I'm not. But I hope you'll come to Laguna, and we can sail again, and ride bikes and walk the beach, just like we always planned."

"I'd love to...once in a while." I couldn't believe I said it, and was still vulnerable enough to hope for a renewal of our lives together. Will I never learn? But there's always a chance, I thought. Maybe we're different, and the year of separation hasn't killed everything we once had.

Denny and I had planned an October trip to see New England in the fall and visit friends in the east. Larry wanted us to begin in Toronto with him, for he had a business trip scheduled that dovetailed with our plans. It seemed like a good idea—perhaps the start of coming closer again. But lingering doubts persisted: why had he forgotten my birthday? I hadn't gotten even a phone call or card. He'd never done that before. Other, minor notes played a discordant melody in my mind. I asked Paul what was happening.

> There is at this time the issue of the tide being neither fully in nor out—you are a piece of sand being washed by your emotions, but you are not your emotions.

> You do not yet fully know in your bones what the separation means: when you feel anger or need or rejection, OBSERVE it. There is great balance and strength in this: you are not denying the emotion or negating the experience, but you are looking at it from a higher perspective.

> You may consider higher in any way you wish, but the way to transcend the pain of this world is to allow the event to occur without the need to alter it by either wish or memory. It be the only means of letting go of the past and finding the glorious future, and

it allows the body to let go of subtle resistance, that slow poison which pollutes the body and bruises the soul.

When the man does disappoint—and he will do so, being encapsulated by his own wants and needs— then observe you, the woman, reacting to the man and allow the drama not to take place inside the body, but in space, where it be possible to let go of the poisoned balloons of anger and fear.

When you float freely without being stuck in a sea of expectations as to what people will do or should do, then it goes well.

There are those who transcend the limitations of this life's troubles. THE WAY TO DO THIS IS BY THE WITNESS OF ONESELF IN THIS LIFE! This is the answer!

Denny and I toured Toronto under cobalt skies. I was excited, for our trip was getting off to a beautiful beginning. Larry took us to dinner, enthused about his business appointments. We were all tired after a busy day and went to our respective beds early.

The next day everything went wrong. Our rental car broke down, it began to rain, and a growing sense of unease was everpresent in me, for I'd heard Larry berate an employee in a voice I'd rarely heard from him: unrestrained anger, wielded by a man accustomed to power. I couldn't shake off my fear in seeing so clearly the coldness in him, even though it hadn't been directed at me...had never been aimed at me in that direct confrontation of man against man. I didn't like what I'd seen, and nothing worked to overcome the pervasive chill.

We went to a tiny, noisy restaurant for dinner. Denny decided to stand in line for tickets at the nearby movie theater.

Larry and I each ordered a glass of wine, and before it arrived, he said, "I think we should start moving toward a divorce."

"What?" I was stunned, sure it was a badly timed joke.

"It just doesn't make sense," he said, very quietly, using the same words I'd heard him yell over the phone the previous night. "It doesn't make sense. We're not doing any better."

For once I was speechless, unable to express the anger that was boiling like an old pot whose fire had been suddenly rekindled. I was sure if I said what I felt, I'd make a fool of myself, and this restaurant was not the place to explode. I had better get control of myself. "Only one thing makes sense," I finally said bitterly. "She finally got to you."

"No. It's not really her, not any more. I think we should start divorce proceedings when we get home. You do it, I guess."

He refused to say any more. I rubbed the glass and looked at the watery rings on the table, thoughts tumbling in my brain. I felt helpless and trapped. I couldn't just get up, pack and fly home in the middle of the night. Where was my responsibility to Denny? How could I leave her—not that she wasn't adult and capable, but we'd planned three weeks together and it was only the second day. What kind of man would spring this at such a terrible time and place? Who was he, anyway? Surely not the man I'd married, but some middle-aged crazy who'd learned to be tough, to take care of himself first.

Denny returned, and looked curiously at the two of us, each silent and ignoring the other. "Still want to go to the movie?" she asked.

I couldn't think of anything better to do at the moment.

We went to the show, I: shivering and shaking in an internal battle between rage and despair, and Larry: able to go to sleep immediately despite the loud soundtrack. His sleeping infuriated me even more.

I spent two more days in Toronto in a state of profound depression and confusion. I was torn between wanting to run home, hide in my bed and pull the covers over my head, and not wanting to ruin the trip Denny and I had so carefully planned. Of course I would go to an attorney when I got home; if I could manage to endure a few more days, Larry would be leaving from Montreal, and I could—perhaps—regain my self-control in the peaceful autumn alone with Denny.

My body reacted with bouts of diarrhea and chills. My hands shook—whether from anger or self-pity, I was never sure.

It was as though we hadn't been separated for a year, and I'd learned nothing from all the growing pains. I thought that the emotions I'd felt for him must have been addiction rather than love, contaminated by memory and distorted by desire. In the midst of the angry feelings, I'd remember an old loving moment and want to hold it to my heart like a flower. I thought I was surely a fool—a weak woman, swayed as always by a man I'd loved, still believing him before trusting myself. Had all of Paul's beautiful words been wasted? Was I doomed to be eternally split between folly and wisdom? I could read his words, and now they felt foreign, neither written nor understood by any part of myself. When it was easier, when I was home, I could read them and something in me could resonate to their peace and believe that I had a gift that enriched me and might someday be shared. Perhaps that, too, was a hoax. No. Never. Not that. It was the best of me, the part that could see through the forest.

I didn't know what to do...and so did nothing.

 *Stranded*

We went from Toronto to Ottawa, an overnight stop, before reaching Montreal. Larry drove, Denny read, and I stared morosely out the window at the endless grey skies, the clumps of foliage just beginning to turn color, scenery uncluttered by billboards.

About two hours past Ottawa, I saw a highway sign for a nearby ranger station. I suggested we go there so I could use the bathroom.

The station was manned by an informative, cheery ranger who seemed happy to be in charge of the vast, flat park area that would soon be covered with snow.

When I went back to the car, Larry was in a phone booth at the edge of the small parking lot and Denny was still curled up in the back seat reading.

"I'm going to take a walk," I said to her. "I need the exercise." I pointed down the road. "I'm going that way. I'll be back in a little while." Denny nodded, and I moved on to pantomime the same message outside the phone booth.

It felt good to stretch my legs and get away from everyone. I walked briskly, breathing deeply, noticing I was walking on the yellow line that divided the narrow, two-lane road. I felt a bit like Dorothy in "The Wizard of Oz"—not that this little walk was going to be adventurous, but feeling that the rest of my life might well be a voyage into the unknown, as this place was unknown. At that thought, loneliness surged in, and I consciously increased my pace and made myself look attentively at the foliage. Both sides of the road were thickly bordered by dank trees, bushes and puddles, and seemed to be more marshland than forest, forcing me to stay on the pavement. The road bent in gentle 'S' curves, and every few hundred yards a small muddy path angled away, ending in a wooden barrier and a posted sign: "NO ADMITTANCE." My camera swung heavily from the neck strap. I'd brought my zoom lens, a heavy one, and it acted as a pendulum unless I cradled camera and lens in the crook of my arm. The scenery, like the sky, was grey and dull. Perhaps I, too, am grey and dull, I thought. I feel as though the life has been beaten out of me. "Change the subject!" I said aloud, and my voice sounded reedy in the silence. The quiet closed in like a fog, and I wondered at the absence of bird cries. I shot a few frames of film to distract me from a creeping uneasiness, and walked on, spotting a dramatic tree at another bend in the road. I had to adjust the exposure, for the day had gotten darker. I'd better go back, I thought. It might rain, and I don't want to ruin my camera.

I turned, and, as if on cue, it began to drizzle. I walked as quickly as I could, awkwardly leaning forward in haste, camera swinging and bumping. I was sure Larry and Denny would round the bend at any moment.

The drizzle changed to rain, and I found a tree that still had a high mantle of protective leaves. The silence had changed to a gentle drumming. I heard a car engine, and felt my heart throb with relief.

An old camper suddenly appeared, heading toward the ranger station. I'd been so sure it was Larry and Denny from the other direction, I never even thought to look behind me.

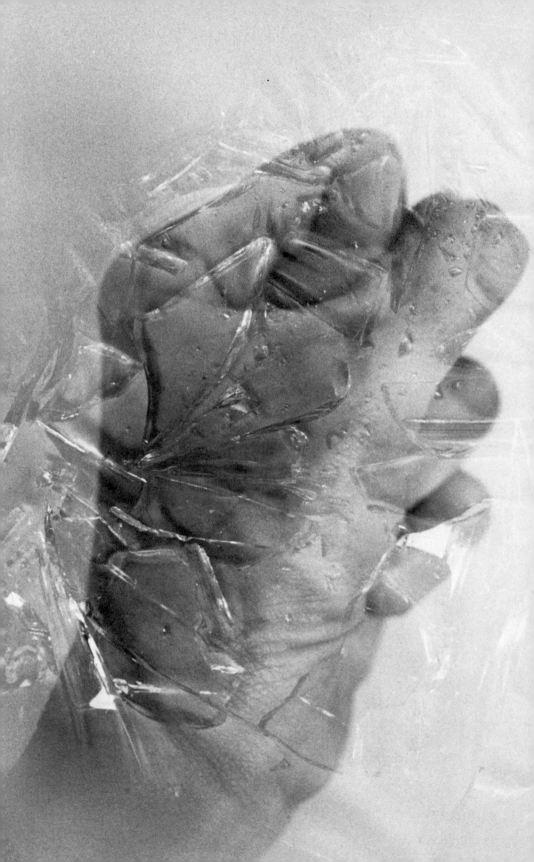

The rain increased as though someone had turned on a shower head to greater velocity. Water poured through the leaves, and there was no better tree to hide under that I could see. I was wet.

I was more than wet...I was furious. Where were they? How dare they be so inconsiderate? Irrational fears swept over me; I felt like a child abandoned by her parents. This was so cruel and mean—nobody loved me. Well, I'd been sure that Denny did, anyway. But nothing was permanent anymore. Surely she couldn't still be reading and not hear the rain? She could easily drive to get me, even if Larry were still on the phone. They ought to bury him with a phone in his ear, I thought bitterly. I was sure he was talking to his future wife, telling her he'd finally dumped me. The ultimate abandonment: husband asks for divorce in foreign country, then leaves wife stranded in the rain in a desolate forest to find her way back to Los Angeles on her own. And I didn't even have a purse—no money. Perfect: just Bobbie and her damn camera, both ruined. I began to cry. How could they do this to me?

More car sounds. Another car, wrong direction. Should I hitch a ride? I'd never done it. What was the worst that could happen? Perhaps I'd be kidnapped, and they'd never see me again. They'll be sorry when I'm gone. Larry would be left with a lot of guilt. Serve him right, too. But Denny wouldn't do this to me. I know she couldn't. I'm sure she wouldn't.

Wet hair was plastered to my head and cold water was dripping under my shirt. I ran to another, bigger tree, and landed in a puddle hidden under a pile of leaves, soaking my tennis shoes.

A low, distant roar grew louder, and I turned and smiled hopefully as two very tough-looking men on a motorcycle zoomed by without so much as a backward glance.

Am I invisible? I thought. I must look so bad nobody even wants to kidnap me! The freeway murderer probably wouldn't even open his door. Nobody wants me. If Larry and Denny ever get here, I won't say a word. I won't complain. I won't condemn. I won't judge. I won't accept their apologies, either. I've never felt so lost and miserable in my life. I've never BEEN so lost and abandoned . . . Wait a minute . . . wait a minute, lady. Number one, I'm not lost. I just haven't been found. I know where the ranger station is, and it isn't that far away. There's a perfectly capable person in there who can offer me a roof, even if he can't get me back home to Los Angeles. And—wet is wet. I'm tired of waiting for someone to rescue me. I'll do it myself. I'd rather walk than sulk. At least it's constructive, and thank God it's not snowing. A St. Bernard with a hot toddy in a keg around his neck sounds more appealing than my family right now. I started to laugh. It sounded loud and strange, but it felt good. I had an instant image of myself writing in a warm, dry room yesterday, asking Paul, "tell me where I am, Paul?" knowing I was at a crossroads in my emotional life, wanting help, as usual. Here was the answer, as graphically as it could be stated: I *was* alone. I'd better get moving on my own and stop the blaming and bitching. I was alive and well, and perfectly capable of walking myself to shelter and warmth. I had put myself on this lovely road, and I could damn well get myself back to safety...or forward, if I so chose.

I walked quickly toward the ranger station, and had only gotten around the next curve when I saw lights coming through the rain. It was not our rental wagon, but the ranger's jeep. He leaned out and smiled, "Get in. You've got a couple of people who've been terribly worried about you. They've been up and down this road for about twenty minutes now, and asked me to help when they couldn't find you."

Larry and Denny rushed out from the station to hug me as I oozed off the car seat. They both began talking at once, telling me how hard they'd looked.

"Please...just get some dry things from my suitcase and the hair blower. We'll talk later. I'm just really cold right now."

Denny went with me to the bathroom and helped blow my hair dry as I shivered into dry clothing. "Oh, mom, we were so worried. Dad was absolutely frantic—I've never seen him like that. We drove up and down that road looking for you."

"But there's only one road. It isn't possible we could have missed each other."

Yet it had happened. They had turned onto every tiny branch, thinking I'd walked into the woods, and were sure I couldn't have gotten as far on the pavement as I had.

"We went three miles down that road," Larry said later, but I didn't believe him. It had only been 3/4 of a mile on the ranger's odometer when we'd measured it and I hadn't walked back that far after I'd turned around.

They'd apparently stopped at the bend before me, and the rain had drowned out their engine and my crying.

Interim

We reached Montreal at last.

I sounded alien in a French-speaking country, and was a stranger to myself: why was I still traveling with a man who had just asked for a divorce. Was he crazy or was I?

In disgust, Denny finally gave up trying to help. She wandered around the cavernous hotel basement to find some amusement in the arcade.

If I can hold out one more day, I thought, I can make it. Denny and I will be on our way to New England, and I'm sure I'll be better once I don't have to look at Larry.

The rain continued, and I stayed in the room, writing, reading, and crying. Paul said,

> *It is so written, as it was always written, that this time with the man be over, and you must be free of him to fully be yourself.*
>
> *In your own mind there has always been a part of him that transcended you. You have many gifts to offer, but not to him at this time. Rejoice. YOU ARE THE GIFT AND GIVER. But it be of necessity for the sad*

218

*woman to retreat into self completely in peace, and
then the coming out be formed well.*

*Be in peace, be in love with the gift of life, for it be
withdrawn from many who savor it more.*

*This be not yet the autumn of your life, but the rich-
ness and warmth of a late summer.*

Once again, the vast gap was evident between the emotional
part of me and a center that was loving.

By not leaving Toronto, I'd made the choice to continue the
trip with Denny. The clock moved slowly until we left. Larry
said, "I'll see you in Boston in two weeks," as though nothing
had happened.

Denny and I crisscrossed New England through a persistent
drizzle, always missing the perfect shot for my cameras. The
trees were late coming into full color and the misty hills and
soggy valleys bore little resemblance to the perfect postcards
of colorful rural scenes. Even the radio in our car refused to
work, leaving us without the distraction of music. Tempers
grew short as the road lengthened. Our quaint country inns
lacked many of the conveniences of home; we found ourselves
stranded in tiny towns, bound like Siamese twins to a soft
double bed that rolled us towards the middle and magnified
my troubled nights.

Twelve days later we drove into Boston as the news of
Anwar Sadat's assassination filled the newspapers.

Denny brightened only at the thought of seeing her best
friend, now going to school in the city. I took the girls to
lunch, my spirits buoyed by their laughter, my mind momentarily off the dread of seeing Larry. That night, they went to
the symphony, and I had dinner with a friend.

Denny and Lauren had obviously had a good chance to talk,
for the next morning they urged me to reconsider the rest of
the trip.

"Mom, give it up. You need to be home in Los Angeles
with your friends. You surely don't need to see Dad. How
can you even look at him?"

"What will you do if I go home?"

"I'll be fine. Lauren says she'd love to go to New York with me, and I'll be in Washington alone. I'd love it! We're not helping each other the way we are now."

"I guess you're right. I *know* you're right."

Denny made plane reservations, I packed hurriedly, and Lauren drove me to the airport. I felt like their child as they encouraged me to take care of myself.

I spent the next two weeks interviewing divorce attorneys, to find one with whom I'd feel most comfortable.

It felt good to be home and seeing Richard again. He always refused to be drawn into discussions about my marital problems. Occasionally it frustrated me, but he was absolutely right...it contaminated our time together.

When the low times slipped in, I turned to Paul.

> *You have chosen this life full of opposites: comfort and pain, dependency and wholeness...look carefully at the last pair, for the truth is that your life will be lived in polarities until you choose to let go of value judgments.*
>
> *There is no gain in making something larger and something smaller, for all creation exists and the parasite that lays low an elephant is therefore as powerful. You will be a pawn of your life if you do not change your point of view to see that ALL that happens is part of a range of possibilities for that situation.*
>
> *Visualize yourself rising above your emotions, your limitations, and it shall be done. You have the power to do this.*

An emergency phone call from Las Vegas left me with a different set of priorities: my father was very ill.

I threw a few things into a suitcase and left immediately.

Dad looked old, sick and helpless. I couldn't speak about my impending divorce during such a desperate time for him, and I resolved at all costs to put on an act of happiness.

I checked him into the hospital and spoke to his doctor about the extensive series of tests that would begin the following day, then walked across the street to my mother's convalescent hospital.

She looked like a pale, wispy cloud blown across an empty sky. She was in diapers and robe, a hopeless mute shell strapped to a chair, awaiting a merciful death. She no longer knew me, could not respond to a presence or a touch. I combed her hair, touched her hand and fled, a sour lump in my throat, trying to find some untapped core of strength in order to keep functioning in a world that was crashing about me.

I felt I was in a war, losing ground in some unseen battle that was out of my control. I could feel myself draining out, with no reserves to deploy, helpless against disasters tumbling forth one after another. I had run from attorney to hospital to hospital to business, trying to maintain a façade of composure and falling apart when alone. The misfortunes left me struggling to keep my sanity, terrified of the future, knowing the pretense of calmness was costing dearly.

A reprieve: the cancer tests were negative, and dad was released to my care at home. Within a week, he was able to make it back to work for a couple of hours a day. I flew home, anxious to see Denny, who had finished her trip and had 'big news.'

We had lunch together. Eyes sparkling, she said, "I'm so excited, Mom! I can't wait to tell you. I'm moving up north— to San Francisco!"

"I'm thrilled for you, honey," I said, lamely. "But I'll miss you terribly—I'm so sorry our trip turned out badly and you were around to mediate our mess."

"When I was alone a lot on the last part of the trip, I realized that I *must* get out of the middle. I need to make my own life and not stay tied to you and dad so much. I do know how much you'd love to have me live in Los Angeles, Mom, but I've got to make this move. I've got to try it."

She was gone within a week, car loaded with everything she could cram in. I found myself at home alone, full of questions to ask Paul:

Paul, this feels like the 'alone time' of which you spoke several months ago. I *am* becoming willing to live alone, to come to know my own strength and power, but I want to know if somewhere in my future I'll find someone with whom I can give and receive love and trust and joy and creativity. I need and want to live on a new plane, a higher plane. I want the loving and the giving and the taking and the fighting and the honesty and the faith and the blooming of this long-hidden flower—which is me—to come into its time.

> *This be a death for each of you, you must know. You need this death to recreate a new life in keeping with the true soul which inhabits the body, and you are to be knowing that this time be for the change-over, and if you be taking it with full teeth and full heart you will find that the path come easier soon, but perhaps not the soonest which is what you be wishing to hear from me.*

Larry continued to call several times a week, always friendly. I refused to see him—it was too painful.

He asked me to delay filing for divorce, saying that changes for the better would be happening in his financial situation and he wished to share that with me. We had always been fair with each other about money, but, generous as it was, his statement didn't ring true. Still, there was nothing to be gained by rushing to speed the divorce proceedings. I told the attorney to wait.

Only once did Larry and I meet; I needed to give back some documents, and he returned some of my personal items. He was quiet and restrained; I was trembling and apprehensive. We sat far apart on our old sofa in my new home. I didn't think I could ever relinquish the familiar curve of his cheek; I wanted to touch him, but would not allow myself to do it. We spoke quietly and wept together. When we walked to the door and he turned to say goodbye, we held each other in a long, lingering hug that encompassed all the years in a tenderness that time had not destroyed. Neither of us could speak.

The girls suggested Christmas Eve dinner. I distrusted my ability to keep my composure, yet the pull to be a family—at least for the holidays—was stronger. I hesitantly agreed.

Denny arrived early in the week with her beloved dog, Linda flew in on the afternoon of the 24th, and Larry drove from his office, small suitcase in hand. He had asked to spend the night so he wouldn't have to drive all the way back to Laguna.

Larry was more subdued than I'd ever seen him; he observed us as though we were actors in a play, and he a remote viewer. It was unnerving to have the familiar, enthusiastic man swallowed up in the watchful, insecure guest, but the truth was that we were all watching each other, measuring our words and actions carefully to eliminate any painful situations.

After dinner we opened family presents; my wariness slipped away and I found myself enjoying the evening more than I thought possible. Larry reached out tentatively several times to touch my hand, like a shy schoolboy on a first date. I pretended not to notice; I didn't know what to do.

At bedtime, we separated to four different areas. Larry took the guest bedroom, Linda slept on the couch, and Denny and dog retreated to the upstairs loft. While I no longer craved Larry's warm body curved around me, my bed felt cold and unnaturally empty. Had I been alone in the house I wouldn't have minded, but sleep came slowly. Still, the evening had been pleasant—even fun at times, and none of the teariness I'd expected had materialized.

After breakfast the next morning, Larry and I decided to walk to the beach. There was a golden clarity in the air—a warm and sunny Southern California Christmas—as children joyously popped out of houses dragging new toys, or careened around cars on first bicycles. Couples walked hand-in-hand through the green ribbon of a park that trimmed the cliff above the Pacific.

"I want you back," he said.

"It's too late. Too late."

"Not for me. I want you. I truly do."

Sarcasm formed thoughts I kept silent. All I managed to say was, "What happened?"

"I hit bottom," he said slowly.

"How do you know when you've hit bottom?" I asked, wondering if he'd allowed any emotion to surface, like bubbles from a sinking ship. I wanted him to feel pain and I needed him to feel the abyss, to know it intimately. Had he raged or cried, or pounded the pillows as I'd done?

"You know when you've hit bottom. When I did, I looked at my life, and realized I had nothing that meant anything without you."

I was silent—too full and too empty to speak.

He drew me into an embrace. I neither resisted nor returned his warmth. Enough years of running the gamut of need, and independence (an unfamiliar feeling) made me unwilling to pretend to be what I no longer was: in love with him. I could hold back my words, but not the doubts that flooded through me. I couldn't believe he'd changed. I only knew that I had, in some deep process that had escaped my daily notice in the turbulence of the last two years.

Larry DID seem to be different, but I had no way of knowing whether the newly sensitive man who listened carefully was temporary or permanent. I mistrusted sudden changes. I was most impressed because he spent no more time selling me on coming back to him.

It was a relief to be alone, and once again I looked forward to a serene time to center and meditate.

One week later, when my father was in Los Angeles for a buying trip, he needed to be rushed to a hospital again, but insisted upon having his own doctor. This time, Larry helped me get him aboard a plane and into a Las Vegas hospital.

Retreat

Once again, by some miracle, dad came through intensive testing with nothing more definite than a severe case of anemia. I took him back to his home, cooked massive amounts of food, and prayed he would soon recover his strength. He was pale and fragile, and unable to take more than a few steps at a time. He couldn't walk up the stairs to his bedroom, so slept on the downstairs sofa. One night, attempting to get up to use the bathroom, he fell across the coffee table and lay sprawled over it, calling weakly for help. I rushed downstairs, but had not the strength to move him. We called the security guard of the building complex at 3 a.m., and the young man tenderly lifted him to his feet.

I found myself drinking coffee all day to keep going, and taking a couple of drinks at night to soothe the jagged edges of pain at seeing him so debilitated. I'll take care of myself later, I thought.

I'd made plans months ago to attend a two-week conference with Brugh Joy, and needed the rest badly. Dad, slowly recuperating, urged me to go. I flew back to Los Angeles, unpacked and repacked in a daze, and drove to Yucca Valley, in the high desert near Palm Springs. I always associated the desert with heat and sun, but I drove into a raw wind and darkening clouds.

The Center for Mentalphysics (what a peculiar name, I thought) was a strung-out cluster of dozens of buildings set on a huge parcel of land studded with joshua trees and laced with dry river beds. Apparently its prime of life had been several decades before, for a couple of the buildings had been designed by Frank Lloyd Wright. I got my room assignment from the registration desk set up in the large cafeteria area, and found the way to my cottage in the deepening twilight.

The small bedroom was filled to capacity by twin beds, a chest of drawers, a nightstand and a chair. I carefully put my things away in half the tiny closet and hoped I'd have a compatible roommate. Two weeks felt like an eternity.

I'd fallen asleep when a knock awoke me. I leapt up to open the door.

My roommate stood in the harsh glare of a lightbulb. She extended her hand and said in an Australian accent, "Hello. I'm Elaine Young." Her smile was brief, her eyes tired.

We spoke as she unpacked. She seemed friendly enough, but worried about the conference. "I had never heard of Brugh Joy," she said, "until a teacher of mine raved on so about him I called and got a last-minute cancellation. I really should be home working, not spending more money here in the States."

"What do you do?"

"I'm a physical therapist. I travel to learn new techniques, new ways of healing people. Oh, I do hope this isn't a mistake to have come."

The next morning at breakfast Brugh welcomed the thirty-six participants and eight assistants. We represented fifteen states and three countries. I couldn't recall ever feeling more distant toward any group. I felt quietly ill; the cumulative effects of all the stress, lack of exercise and poor diet had crept up on me and demanded to be noticed.

The first working session began at 9:30 a.m. in an immense meeting hall. Our pillows, set in a circle, were dwarfed by the dimly lit space. Behind Brugh was a complex stereo and recording system, with four speakers set about us. As he'd done nearly three years before at his ranch, he began now by playing classical music at high volume as we lay on the floor. I fell asleep and was nudged awake by a neighbor who whispered pleasantly, ''You're snoring.''

In his introductory talk, Brugh said ''Nothing is required of you except that you not be in contact with the outer world. No phone calls, no television, no radio, no trips to town. It will be a rare time in which you can experience yourselves without the usual distractions that life always provides.'' I knew I'd cheat and call dad, but it was the only way I could attend the conference without being overtaken by guilt.

Brugh added, ''You're not required to attend our sessions or meals if whatever is going on in you feels more important. This is the time for you to observe the larger patterns within your life without judging them, and without comparing yourself to others. It's critical that you do not limit or reduce your experiences by intellectualizations. The processes we will be doing are designed to enhance new awareness. I'm not minimizing the difficulty in letting go of your rational mind; I'm providing you with a setting in which you can most easily explore and go deeper into your own processes. Just know that you have, for perhaps the only time in your life, the perfect place in which to discover the vast richness of yourselves in an infinite universe of possibilities.''

I wanted only to sleep, to free my mind from churning with concern about dad's future and my response to Larry's wanting me back. The issues pervaded every thought, contaminated every peaceful moment.

I told Elaine my situation, and the need to stand back to look at my life in a new perspective.

We spoke of our children, our lives as wives and mothers, and the trials of being single when no longer young. We found that living on two different continents had not precluded many common experiences.

''I used to be married,'' she said. ''My husband left me with four young daughters and I had to go to work. Actually, it was the best thing that could have happened to me, although I didn't think so at the time.''

She offered to give me a therapy treatment, and I accepted gladly.

It was quite different from anything I'd ever had. She put a small box on my stomach, then connected a wire between it and her ear. She began at my head by gently stroking my hair and face with motions so delicate it was as though she held a feather in her hands. I'd never been so utterly mesmerized by a touch; I felt like a small child being soothed and comforted. There was no massage as such, which is what I'd expected—rather, long flowing moves that brushed away cobwebs of tension. She seemed to know precisely how long to stay in each area, as though she were reading my body.

When it was over I asked her how she knew what I was thinking.

"The box," she smiled. "Your stomach gurgles told me very plainly."

"I didn't hear a thing," I said.

"That's the idea. I hear it, you relax. I must say, you have a very, very sensitive body, and it responded beautifully."

Whether it was the power of suggestion or not, I felt much better after that.

My days began at 5:30 a.m. with a hot shower to prepare me for the freezing pre-dawn walk to the chapel. I bundled up against the intense cold, enjoying the changing light as sunrise backlit the mountains to the east and stars faded from the sky. The pale red glow of dawn illuminated the land and its sparseness; in the glittering clarity it seemed to be waiting with a spiny patience.

The chapel was a simple, elegant building designed by Frank Lloyd Wright's son in his father's tradition. Inside, on either side of a square open area clustered with prayer stools and a large Tibetan gong, were small cubicles, each enclosed on three sides by partitions and on the fourth by a curtain. I loved the solitude, felt I was in my private cave, and arranged myself comfortably on cushions as I attempted to still my active mind, churning with mind chatter despite the quiet walk.

Brugh had shown us a technique that I was sure would help me meditate more successfully—to achieve that stillness of mind in which the world opens and new perspectives present themselves effortlessly.

One morning I became unusually still. My body found a comfortable place and did not call attention to itself. No effort was involved. My mind seemed content to remain in a blank cavern instead of wandering to the troubled past or an unknown future. As though I were watching a movie, I saw through closed eyes a slow procession coming to a halt on the desert floor. One figure was gently laid on the blistering, shimmering sand. The others moved away, disappearing like a mirage. The faceless figure was scalded through its torn rags; its feet were raw and bloody. Unseeing eyes stared at the red ball of the sun, and its mouth opened, gasping for air, the tongue a swollen, parched torment. The body was dying in excruciating pain. Suddenly I understood that *I* was that figure, that this had really happened—and was still happening to me, although I knew myself to be sitting in a cool, dark room. I saw myself being stung by insects, ravaged by ants, watched by animals waiting to move in for the kill. The terror was real, yet removed. I knew—without knowing how I knew—that I observed from one dimension as my death occurred in another. There was no time. As the soul in that body and in mine were one, I experienced what death must be: relief, release from all that binds us to this restless planet and to limited bodies and minds. *Death was freedom.* There was a breathless pause as the creatures watched in silence and the blazing sun instantly became a starry night. The pain stopped, and the body—my body—merged into the sand to become one with the land and its inhabitants. To feed them, as I had fed from them, was suddenly acceptable. The process of life, death and decay was no longer terrifying, but a natural progression to Source. An enormous peace enfolded me.

I had no idea how long the imagery had lasted.

At some deep level, I knew I'd witnessed this scene to free me from a frightening death experience in another lifetime that had left some residue in memory. I might never be able to explain it satisfactorily to anyone, but it was, nevertheless, intensely real.

When I left the chapel the sun was up. The desert appeared new and different. Early morning frost glistened on each plant, and the cacti had a thousand glittering fingers pointing out-wards and upwards.

Brugh had asked us to bring a cassette player and some blank tapes, primarily to record our dreams while still half-asleep and able to remember them. Many people reported incredibly vivid dreams, full of symbolism that I was unable to decipher. Several times I heard Elaine, in her precise accent, speaking very softly into her recorder.

I knew I dreamt, but could rouse myself to record only a few. They were singularly dull and not worth mentioning in the group; Larry was in every dream, often surrounded by women. I was usually on the fringe, watching him and feeling unhappy.

Asleep or awake, feelings about him cropped up as suddenly as rabbits broke from hiding and disappeared down a hole. I wanted to be free of everyone, especially Larry, but he was everywhere. I was unwilling to be stuck in old reactions, and I was not yet capable of creating new ones. I didn't know how to sort out my mixed feelings to his presence in my life again. I was more confused than ever.

One morning I went to the chapel as usual after recording a worrisome dream that had awakened me, but couldn't seem to quiet my mind, which was insistently repeating some angry moments with Larry.

Brugh had said, "If you can't get your linear mind to quiet down, sometimes you can calm it effectively with a trick. Tell your mind to go fill a large hall with people to whom you can tell your story. Charge admission! Make it as real as you can, complete the scenario, and then leave yourself the space to retreat peacefully into meditation."

It seemed as good a suggestion as anything else I could think of, so I settled down a little more comfortably against the cushions in my cubicle, and imagined that I'd brought hun-dreds of friends and acquaintances here to Yucca Valley to hear the whole drama about our marriage, separation, and impending divorce...from my viewpoint, of course. I saw myself posing dramatically before a large, faceless group, and beginning my litany of injustices. Suddenly, they all got to their feet and said in unison, "We're bored! We're tired of the whole story! Get on with your life and shut up about the past!" and walked out en masse. The scene struck me as hilarious—and so true—I broke into raucous laughter and heard a sibilant "shhhhhhh!" from the other side of the curtain. A silent chuckle bubbled in my throat, and although I couldn't get into a meditative state, the point wasn't lost. The imagery became all the more meaningful for being laced with humor.

That night it poured, with great beating streams of water cascading down the buildings. Cold, wild winds threatened to wrench the plants from their tenuous moorings in the sand, and tumbleweeds blew in great bounces across the desert, only to become impaled on cacti.

The next morning, scattered puddles of ice on the sand lent an unreal dimension to the scene. The day stayed chilly and the ice did not melt in the shady places. The crispness and smell of the frigid air was exhilarating; after our group meeting, I walked to my favorite place, a dry stream bed that was etched into the desert floor.

Great scudding clouds formed, tore apart, and reformed, casting fast-moving shadows on the land; the wind made every joshua tree into a groaning, beckoning soul trapped in a spiny form. The desert was alive with scurrying animals burrowing new homes. My heavy hiking boots opened great holes of footprints in the moist sand, and I felt as though I were being pulled down to an underground lake by an unseen hand. The stream bed had become a many-branched thing, deeply incised and lined with the torn debris of plants clinging to clotted pieces of soil. Only the styrofoam cups, shotgun shells, and rusting beer cans were out of place, needing time to grind down their intrusion.

I sat on a broken branch that formed a jutting seat, and looked up. Birds coasted on invisible currents of air, framed against the subtle cloud colors and the patched deep blue sky. I'd always wanted to nestle in a cloud, supported by the wind, and feel us turn silver, lilac, rose...feel the freedom to form, disperse, reform, dissolve. If I rode the wind, where would we end? Dashed to pieces on a mountain, splintered and down-drafting? Or did the wind curl back upon itself like a wave, to come together to form a giant moving band around the earth like the trades?

I felt like a bird about to leave the nest, frightened and daring all at once, not knowing whether I'd fly or fall. I thought I saw my pattern, plain as a jet trail, brushed against the sky.

I could read it easily: I'd circled and circled my past—this valley—through memory and response. I'd needed to depend on what *had* happened in order to predict what *would* happen. I'd needed to feel I had CONTROL over my life to feel secure. Suppose I gave that up for freedom to act in the present tense? Could I? I knew I'd bound myself to the past, because the known seemed safer than the unknown. I'd confined myself to a small territory; if I could fly free of memory, to follow the wind wherever it blew—away from the life and man I'd known, or perhaps back to him, with strong wings to make it new, I'd be living on the wind, trusting it would support me if I soared or struggled against it. I'd learned to trust Paul, and he'd brought me sustenance in crisis and reliance on my inner voice. If I flew with the wind, instead of circling this valley again and again, I'd fly over the mountains, daring to rise over the rim to an unseen land, a green and fertile place.

The imagery cleared to nothingness—no feelings, no thoughts, no visions. I was all alone on my branch, content to do nothing, to be no more than I was. The I that was known to me and the inner voice that was often a surprise merged with the wind and the clouds, the past and the future.

The sun changed position, the clouds rearranged themselves, and I came back to a body that needed to rest in a warm, cozy room.

One night, Brugh announced that he would do a 'balancing' on each of us, at a specific time and day, and we were to bring our favorite cassette of music.

When I arrived for my appointment, the meeting hall held four massage tables placed near the center of the room. At either end of each table was an assistant, one of them my group leader, Lyn, who motioned me to lie down. Headphones were placed on my ears, I heard the soothing notes of *Ecstasy*, and the assistants began a gentle routine of subtle touch. My eyes closed, and I ebbed into relaxation, breathing gently.

Vision wasn't necessary to sense Brugh's energy as he approached the table. I felt the intense heat of his hand through my sweater as he delicately touched a point on the midline of my body on the rib cage. The heat penetrated every part of me. There was no sound, other than the music playing softly on the headphones. I felt like a musical instrument with thousands of wires, each being finely adjusted and tuned to a new, more harmonious pitch. I heard myself let go of a huge sigh that emptied all the pent-up sadness from my body. I floated on a stream of rippling peace.

I knew when he moved away by the absence of heat. I was gently covered with a warm blanket.

I awakened to the sound of the dinner bell clanging, and tried to sit up quickly, but could not. My body didn't want to leave the blissful, passive state, but I remembered that I had kitchen duty and needed to help the staff set out the evening meal.

After Brugh had balanced everyone, over a span of several days, he asked for our comments. Everyone had a different response, ranging from, "I felt nothing at all," to "It was one of the most extraordinary things that's ever happened to me!"

Changes

The days moved on in a gentle cadence. At many sessions, Brugh introduced some concept to practice which increased the awareness of our inner self. Many of the exercises came from his book, *Joy's Way*, which I had read several years before. I needed to read it again, and found passages I couldn't recall, as though a part of me hadn't understood what he said and remembered nothing.

I was in awe of his intellect, philosophy and the clarity with which he presented ideas and I felt incredibly fortunate to be learning from him.

The group still seemed to be a strange mix of personalities. Perhaps I was the only one feeling so antisocial; still, it felt appropriate to be less a talker than a listener—not my usual pattern.

Among the participants were five doctors, one a young surgeon who reminded me of Larry. Bob was suffering the pains and fears of a terminal disease: amyotrophic lateral sclerosis—Lou Gehrig's disease. The usual course was progressive paralysis, helplessness, and death, generally through paralysis of

234

the respiratory system. Medicine held no cure, and his court of last resort was Brugh and the metaphysical, holistic process, which held that beliefs can cause both illness and healing.

Bob was desperately seeking answers and refusing to look at the *pattern* of his life; the dichotomy was not lost on me, for it seemed we all did that to some degree: begged for solutions, pleading: "help me!" yet took no responsibility for the problem. Shown a pattern, whatever it might be, we ignore changing the structure, clinging like a barnacle to what we've built, wondering why serenity and health are never ours. Bob was a mirror for us. I was sure that most were here for answers, even if we couldn't always verbalize the questions.

I saw some parallels between Bob and Larry. Both were successful and hard-working, reared to have high standards and to be 'the best,' with definite rules of behavior and morality. Bob's parochial background had labelled many impulses as 'sins,' but he admitted that there was a growing part of him that wanted to be free of all responsibility, although he loved his wife and children, medical practice and service to the community. He felt under a great deal of pressure to be everything to everyone. Larry had wanted freedom from the confinement of marriage, denying his feelings for a long time, channeling energy into business and pretending everything was wonderful. Both men found it difficult to look within, repressing every thought that didn't conform to what they "should" be, not admitting the humanness of their distress or the rigidity of their responses...the sin/guilt ways of perceiving the world. Both suffered from diseases which caused symptoms of rigidity in the body while the mind denied any connection to the physical distress; the disease had just 'happened' to them.

I had come to believe that we don't have to live out all our fantasies so much as *honor* them as being a part of ourselves. Our culture doesn't teach understanding that part of us often wants what is forbidden. To experience our dark side in an inner process and to know that we don't necessarily have to indulge our desires, but recognize and permit them to have a real—if interior—existence, is growth.

Midway through our two-week conference, Brugh announced that we'd have sixty hours of fasting and silence, extending after the midday meal on Sunday to breakfast Wednesday morning. No group sessions or meetings would be held, but the recreation room, Friendship Hall, would be open twenty-four hours a day with juices, herb teas, coffee, and a place to be with others without talking. We were requested not to play music or get involved with a book, other than our own writings, to allow the period of self-examination as few diversions as possible. Brugh added, ''This is the time and place to do your personal ritual, whatever that may be. Allow yourself to fully experience this special time: you're not being deprived, just encouraged to go inward.''

I was concerned. I had never fasted, and my low blood sugar condition didn't allow for skipped meals—I was sure I'd feel faint or light-headed. When extremely hungry, I could be more than irritable; if food wasn't accessible, the physical pain in my stomach provoked anger. I mentioned it to Brugh, who smiled and as usual said nothing, leaving it to the individual to solve the problem. I knew if I got desperate there was a refrigerator packed with goodies. Bob needed to take his potent medications with food, so Brugh certainly allowed exceptions for medical reasons. Was I one? Everyone else I spoke to readily accepted the idea of fasting, and many had done it before.

I decided to talk to my stomach. I sat on a chair, looked down, and said aloud, feeling both silly and sincere: ''I really want your cooperation. I know you can go through the fasting feeling healthy, and I'M GIVING YOU MY FULL, LOVING PERMISSION TO DO SO.'' I heard a growl from below my belt.

Brugh had set up a juicer in the Friendship Hall kitchen, and provided fifty-pound sacks of fresh carrots nearby. I noticed one of the men processing enough for a large glass of juice, and followed his example. It was amazingly satisfying. Once I got used to the *idea* that I could be perfectly healthy without solid food, one or two glasses of carrot juice substituted nicely for a meal. I stayed away from coffee, and found a lemon wedge squeezed in a glass of fresh water was refreshing and somewhat filling.

I thought that time would begin to drag, but in fact the hours were like jewels.

When hunger crept in, I walked to the Hall—about ten minutes away—prepared the juice and sat in a chair near the big fireplace blazing with warmth. There were always people studying Tarot cards or the I Ching book Brugh had introduced us to. He said it could help free our minds from linear thought processes.

If I was tired, I slept. If not, I walked and watched the desert. It felt like years since I had to rush.

The chapel was always open. I went at an unaccustomed hour, at night, and fell into a deep, refreshing sleep on the floor when meditation didn't come.

"It's wonderful," I wrote later, "not to care about time. And, most of all, not to have to do anything or be anything."

One night, I was attracted to some kindling I saw near the big woodpile. I picked up a dozen of the smaller pieces and began to construct something near the hearth. I made several trips outdoors for more blocks of varied sizes, and a building formed: a house of many rooms with a cardboard roof. I was fascinated—the hours flew by, and I fantasized about being the architect of this Parthenon of Kindling. I found crayons, and drew on some of the blocks, neither knowing nor caring about anything but the pleasure of creation. When imagination stepped aside and allowed mind to control, it said, "I want to keep it forever! It's MINE! I want everyone to appreciate this beautiful piece of work!" I moved away to get a glass of water, then came back and toppled my palace, knowing it was an appropriate time to let go of the need for recognition and attachment to what I'd done. I was stronger for destroying it.

I rarely saw Elaine. She chose to sleep in the Hall, curled up in a sleeping bag on an old sofa, and I relished the privacy. When we passed on a path, we hugged in silence, and felt our hearts beating in unison beneath the warm sweaters. I noticed others using touch to communicate friendship, and began to enjoy the silence even more.

My body felt lighter and better than it had in years, with energy and focus to pursue ideas. I had no gnawing hunger, only a little lightheadedness that passed in an afternoon.

I'd wondered what my ritual would be. On Tuesday morning I knew, without doubt, remembering as I planned it a lonely little girl pretending to be an Indian, needing to feel powerful, always feeling 'different.'

I prepared carefully, lovingly. I looked for feathers, but found none. In my backpack I put a tie, scarf, pantyhose, bedroom slippers that looked like moccasins, lipstick, crayons, and kindling. I set out for a hill I'd seen in the distance but hadn't climbed. It appeared to have a commanding view of the valley and a difficult, short, hike to the top. I named it 'Larry.'

Near the base, I wondered if there wasn't a simpler way than a hand-over-hand climb of the boulders tumbled below the pinnacle. There was no need to hurry, so I circled behind and found an easy path. The view was all I thought it would be.

There was a small, flat area—exactly the space I wanted for my ritual. I undressed and roared with laughter as I redressed as a male Indian: tied the line around my waist and looped the scarf over it as a loincloth might look. I put on the moccasins, painted my face with lipstick, and tied the pantyhose around my head like a headband, the dangling feet becoming drooping feathers. It was utterly absurd—and delicious! I wondered if one could become drunk from lack of food.

Once my laughter subsided, I was aware of my being both feminine and masculine, in a way I'd not felt before. The masculine felt powerful and proud, ready to lead and sure of knowledge gained in a lifetime of listening to nature. The feminine was wise in a different way: more passive, but no less sure; vulnerable but nurturing, acknowledging the aspect that needed to show strength.

I sat down on a slab of rock, wincing at the cold, gritty surface and took out the kindling pieces and began to draw and write on them. I wanted to make a small fire—not because of the warmth, for it was a balmy day, for a change—but for the power of it. Fires were forbidden, so I imagined one, stood up and faced north, the first stick in my hands, held upright to the summit of the sky.

"To you, North, I honor Wisdom—and its shadow side, Ignorance. If I had not been ignorant, I would not have sought wisdom." I paused, and felt into the words I said aloud before putting the stick on the ground.

With the second stick, I faced west. "To you, West, I honor Creativity, and its shadow, Conformity." I thought of all the times I'd taken the easy way rather than working through a situation with an open mind, to see what was true for me. I thought that creativity had less to do with projects than with an attitude toward life: "looking with new eyes at each day like an animal just borned," as Melle had said so long ago, knowing change is an essential part of creativity.

I picked up the third painted stick and faced south. "I honor Illumination, and its counterpart, Righteousness, knowing that when I move from a place of judgment and limited vision —contraction—I become open to *that which is:* expansion."

I held the fourth stick high, and thought long before saying out loud: "I honor you, East: you are Trust. I know all too well your dark side, Control. Both of you are fully present in my life, and I assume, always will be. I know I have a choice, not a battle, between you two."

I felt in balance, in harmony; I knew that the reverse was imbalance: *dis-ease.* I saluted my body which had sustained the life in me when my emotional self had not cared whether I lived or died. I was like a fountain of gratitude for what had been given and what had not been taken, and sat down once again on the boulder to reflect on the valley below.

There was a moment of perfect repose, followed by a strong need to be recognized for having done a very special ritual.

Recognized, for God's sake! I thought. Is there no end to relearning the lessons?

When the fasting and silence drew to a close, I knew I'd never had such perfect freedom. There had been no deprivation, just opportunity to listen to the self—the silly, wise, demanding, reaching, listening part that had played its many roles without needing to pretend to be anything other than what it was. It was a time of *being.* Words limited the experience.

The need to define my future relationship with Larry disappeared. I knew I had the ability to make the best decision— whatever that might be. The woman I'd become had different needs from the girl who had married the man of her dreams. I no longer needed to be dependent upon a relationship for my self-realization; the years of learning to trust the inner voice had slowly brought me to this point: my responsibility to sustain myself as a loving, strong, serene woman, able to face the world on its terms—not my demands.

Silence had been a wonderful gift. I knew it had a spatial quality, allowing time to alter and slowing or stopping the inner chatter so that a new rhythm was heard, one more in harmony with the higher self. Silence had more sensitivity in it than most speech, and touch was so expressive. I had come to know people by a smile or a hand on the shoulder.

As the conference drew to a close, I felt a clear change from the anxious, tense woman who'd arrived nearly two weeks earlier. It was a different process than 'finding answers' to problems: I knew myself in a new and vital way, aware that such knowledge was not a summation, but an ongoing eternal process.

I knew that 'the real world' would once again present its tests and traumas, but I felt an ability to look at them with inner eyes that had seen the larger pattern of my life, and would know how to ride the winds.

Epilogue

Honolulu, January 1983. Nearly a year since our renewal—an appropriate time and place to assess how we are, where we're going.

We have just strolled by the yacht harbor, had breakfast in the coffee shop, and read the morning paper in shared silence, looking like the long-banded couple we are once again.

Larry has left for work in his colorful Hawaiian shirt, briefcase in hand. He is a man filled with love, still in awe of our renaissance and no longer needing to pretend to be perfect. Business is still a battle and a joy for him, but no longer overwhelms the part that needs rest and renewal.

Emotions come to the surface and we talk about our feelings with ease. Larry and I look at each other with new eyes, each seeing a face grown more dear with time. We know no person can be all to another and we're enjoying our differences rather than denying them. We have found new ways to laugh at our mistakes, at each other, instead of blaming; a new tolerance for the gaps we balance so well when we are centered and easy within ourselves.

How did we come to this wondrous point in our lives? That we are here, is enough. Perhaps the pain cleansed instead of

241

soured us, for we live each day in appreciation of the other, rarely dwelling on the past, and planning for a future in which we continue to share our love and bounty in an ever-widening circle.

I dare not ask if it will linger: to demand that it does would be to destroy its precious fragility, like a bubble burst by a poking finger. We teeter on the brink of new discoveries, of falling into old chasms, and walk the Way hand in hand.

I am alone in our hotel room that overlooks the concrete corridor of the city, sitting at the typewriter, waiting for words to describe the miracle of our togetherness.

Taking inventory of me, giving myself the full, loving permission to become more than I am, is as much as I can manage. After the hilly years, my life seems to be at a plateau. It is a welcome, comfortable resting spot.

I continue—sporadically, as always—to ask Paul for guidance, and value his help. I accept it as a guidepost in my life and believe that each of us has a ''voice'' in some form. My inner self tells me it is not the time for me to instruct or heal others, beyond what a reader may find in this book, for I am still in a tender, healing state...not quite ready to move on to the next phase of my life—whatever that may be.

I believe psychic phenomena to be signs on the road to consciousness. To linger long in their shadow is to delay progress, for they seduce a traveler into thinking he has found the rainbow at the end of the path, when, in fact, he is just beginning.

The road is each lifetime's journey toward harmony and wholeness. Only when we honor *all* that we are—the male and female in each of us, and the dark as well as the light—can we integrate body, mind and spirit and be free to change and expand, rather than condensing ourselves into tight balls of protectiveness.

I feel that each of us can find our center: that real place of knowingness which works toward our enlightenment and exalts our life. By *intent* we do move to discover it, and by action do we fan this life-force into a positive, loving flame which enriches ourselves and our world.

By acknowledging our need to return to this center when we are out of balance, we affirm joy and find our divinity.

For autographed copies of

RETURN TO CENTER

Send your order to:

Bobbie Probstein
P.O. Box 1433
Santa Monica, CA 90406-1433

Please enclose your check or money order for $12.90 per copy
($10.95 plus $1.95 postage and handling); California residents
please add prevailing sales tax.